COME AND SEE – THE STORY OF LOURDES

Micheál Liston is a native of Banogue, Co. Limerick. Ordained for the Limerick Diocese in 1968, he has worked in parish work as curate and parish priest. He was director of the Apostolate of Youth in the diocese for fifteen years, and now helps out pastorally and administratively in the west Limerick pastoral area of Íde Naofa, and in a number of school chaplaincies. Articles of his have appeared in pastoral magazines and he has had a book of poetry in Irish published, *Screadfaidh na Clocha Amach*.

COME *and* SEE

THE STORY *of* LOURDES

MICHEÁL LISTON

VERITAS

Published 2013 by Veritas Publications
7–8 Lower Abbey Street
Dublin 1, Ireland
publications@veritas.ie
www.veritas.ie

ISBN 978-1-84730-509-1

10 9 8 7 6 5 4 3 2 1

The lines from 'Advent' and 'Having Confessed' by Patrick
Kavanagh are reprinted from *Collected Poems*, edited by Antoinette
Quinn (Allen Lane, 2004), by kind permission of the Trustees
of the Estate of the late Katherine B. Kavanagh, through the
Jonathan Williams Literary Agency.

A catalogue record for this book is available from the British
Library.

Designed by Heather Costello, Veritas Publications
Printed in Ireland by Hudson Killeen Limited, Dublin

FOREWORD

THE EXPERIENCE OF LOURDES 'GROWS ON YOU'. IT IS NO accident that Canon Micheál Liston refers several times to the example of Mary who 'treasured all these words and pondered them in her heart' (Lk 2:19).

Pilgrims in Lourdes often learn to ponder and to recognise that the time they spend there is not just a few days of withdrawal from real life. The experience is more real than much of the great buzz of competing priorities that claim our attention most of the time. In their pilgrimage they find new insights into those daily concerns and perhaps learn to look at their priorities in a new light.

Lourdes shows the Church and the world as they ought to be. The sick and the people who carry great burdens of anxiety, people who sometimes feel overwhelmed or marginalised, discover that in Lourdes it is they who have the first place. The joy and vitality of young people and of other volunteers are cheerfully at the service of the sick and the frail.

In Lourdes, people whose lives are filled with responsibilities, with the bustle of modern life, with the hardships of a world in recession, with personal and family anxieties, can take time to reflect quietly in the peaceful atmosphere of the grotto or in the presence of the Blessed Sacrament. They can meet the generous mercy of God in the Sacrament of Reconciliation. In those moments of prayer they can learn, not least from the example of Bernadette, that we are loved by a God who has in store for us things that no human eye has seen nor ear heard nor human heart conceived (cf. 1 Cor 2:9).

This book is the fruit of many years during which the author has pondered in his heart the story of Lourdes and the experience of being a pilgrim in Lourdes. It is the work of someone who is passionate about the story of a young, frail, uneducated girl who met the Blessed Virgin and who gave her account of that meeting with humility, confidence, integrity and consistency in the face of scepticism and ridicule.

During Limerick diocesan pilgrimages to Lourdes, one of the highlights is the 'walking tour' in which Canon Micheál shares his enthusiasm and his reflections about Lourdes and the story of Bernadette with pilgrims who are enthralled by the richness of what they hear.

This book will tell that story and communicate that enthusiasm to a new audience. The first part gives a full and thoughtful account of what occurred. The second part presents a series of rich reflections on topics ranging from the wonder of being made in the image of God, to the meaning of Our Lady's call to repentance which many people initially find off-putting, to the place of the sick in Lourdes and in our lives, to the hope which many people find during their pilgrimage.

I hope that this book will bring light and serenity to many people and that it will encourage readers to share the sense of wonder, and the awareness of God at work through Mary and Bernadette, which so evidently inspire the author. This is, in the proper sense of the word, a 'heartfelt' work and I am confident that it will, in its turn, touch the hearts of those who read it.

✠ Donal Murray
Bishop Emeritus of Limerick

ACKNOWLEDGEMENTS

I AM GRATEFUL TO THE LIMERICK DIOCESAN Pilgrimage, directors, staff and all involved with it, for their inspiration, support and companionship over the years. In particular I wish to acknowledge my debt to Canon Donal McNamara and Fr Joseph Noonan. I wish also to acknowledge my appreciation of the service and courtesy of Fr Brian de Búrca, chaplain of the sanctuary of Lourdes, and all who animate the wonder that is Lourdes as a source of peace for so many in our human family. I wish to express my gratitude to Veritas for inviting me to write this book. In particular I am grateful to Donna Doherty for her wisdom, competence and patience. My friends Gearóid Ó Tiarnaigh and Frank Prendergast have been generous with their encouragement and practical help. I also wish to express appreciation to work colleagues for their understanding and support. It was in the context of home and extended family that I first heard the story of Lourdes, and I hope this book will be a celebration of a heritage we share with so many.

In memory of all those who have travelled on the Limerick Diocesan Pilgrimage to Lourdes.

CONTENTS

INTRODUCTION

FOR OVER 150 YEARS, MILLIONS OF PEOPLE HAVE BEEN drawn to the grotto in the small town of Lourdes at the foot of the Pyrenees in the south of France. The sick and those in need come. The devout and the curious come. Maybe it is better not to speculate too much about people's motivation. The fact is that people are drawn to this place for their own reasons, responding to an invitation to 'come and see'.

In 1913, the Bishops of Ireland organised the first Irish National Pilgrimage to Lourdes. Before that, smaller groups and individuals were already making their way to the shrine. Today individuals, families, parishes, dioceses and all kinds of Church groups continue to respond to the wonder that is Lourdes.

As regards the facts of Lourdes, I think it is important to state that we have an enormous amount of documentation even from the time of the apparitions – February 1858 to July of that year. The Benedictine scholars, René Laurentin and Bernard Billet, in their work *Lourdes: Documents Authentiques* (seven volumes, 1956–66), assembled a challenging amount of material, covering the period from the birth of Bernadette in 1844 to her departure for the convent in Nevers in 1866. Ruth Harris, a historian in Oxford, says that these scholars 'sought to end historiographical dispute once and for all by providing a truly "scientific" history stripped of the rancour of the past. The monumental works they produced did indeed quell all serious controversy over the facts ...'[1] For those who want to go deeper into the facts of Lourdes I would strongly recommend the work of René Laurentin and Bernard Billet, and Ruth Harris.

From my own first contact with the pilgrimage centre, I was drawn by the popular nature of the place, with so many people from so many different places, so at ease with what was happening. What drew me into exploring the origins of the pilgrimage was the way its emphasis on penance made me a bit uncomfortable. The call to a change of heart is still a radical call, maybe now more than ever. Still, I think I now have a better grasp of the healing and the joy that God is offering. Also, the peace, goodwill and hope in a place where so much human suffering is gathered is indeed something wonderful.

In the first section of this book I have told the story of Lourdes as I am still discovering it. So much of what I am learning centres around the idea of communion, or shared life, which is the central idea of the call to renewal of the Second Vatican Council. In Lourdes we are offered an experience of what that means in the flesh. Another idea of the Vatican Council was that the Church is God's field, a cultivated field.[2] I start the story with the idea that the parish of Lourdes in 1858 was a

---

1. Ruth Harris, *Lourdes: Body and Spirit in the Secular Age*, London: Penguin, 2000, p. 20.

2. Cf. *Lumen Gentium*, 6.

cultivated field, yes, but an under-cultivated field, like every other parish.

In the second section I have tried to reflect on the reality of Lourdes in a way that celebrates its vigour and its continuing attraction for people today. A lot of people today want to explore faith issues in the context of experience. Lourdes helps us feel and imagine what faith, hope and love can be in the flesh.

Part One

THE STORY OF LOURDES

Lourdes Before the Apparitions

A FEW YEARS AGO THERE WAS A SMALL FIELD belonging to a parish that was rather uncared for and definitely neglected. Once a year, a neighbour cut the grass in it for his cows and that was that. Things rested so until as part of a general renewal of parish and community life, a community garden was considered. Now this same small field is producing vegetables and fruits and flowers and all kinds of things that are good to eat and to look at. People in the community who were considering growing more of their own food have been encouraged and supported, while they in turn support the project. People on community employment schemes have benefitted. Produce from the garden has been sold and the money given to famine relief.

This story of the development of one parish's community garden, though quite different in scope to the establishment of Lourdes as a great centre of prayer and pilgrimage, parallels the story of Lourdes all the same in involving the grace of God working with the local parish.

At the beginning of spring 1858, no one in the parish of Lourdes and the diocese of Tarbes had any idea of what was going to emerge among them that Lent and Easter. We might say they had enough worries of their own besides thinking about what part they might be asked to play in God's plans. For many, life was hard. In deteriorating economic conditions, some struggled to find enough to eat or to find shelter from the elements. Work was not easy to come by and money was scarce. Still, it was a community with resources of humanity and Christian faith, with neighbourliness and courage.

Situated at the foothills of the Pyrenees, between France and Spain, Lourdes in the 1850s was a town of about 4,000 people, the local town for the area of Bigorre. An 800-year-old castle on the highest point of the town signifies the relative importance of the place in the past. About 120 men of the town were regarded as notables – men in the liberal professions, people of property, physicians and so on. Most of the population are on the highest point of it made up of farmers, shepherds, millers, forestry workers and workers in the stone quarries. At the bottom of the social spectrum were those who tried to get a day's work wherever they could, earning the meagre sum of 1.20 francs a day.

The turmoil of the French Revolution reached Lourdes, and the area suffered during Napoleon's wars in Spain. The new ideas of the Enlightenment had their supporters among the notables – those involved in the civil administration of the town and surrounding area, as well as in the local press. So while the people living at the foothills of the Pyrenees went about their daily lives, many factors were beginning to encroach on their circumstances and many different influences beginning to compete for their attention.

Most of the people and all the poorer people spoke a local language, Bigourdan, through which they were in touch with a rich local, traditional culture that enabled them to live in the particular conditions of their place and time. Their folklore included a great store of stories of otherworldly creatures, saints and demons. So, in contrast to the new stories of enlightenment and the triumph of reason coming among them, there was this access to their own traditions and to a broader culture of the Pyrenees that gave them an affinity with the Spanish side of the mountains.

The local Christian community was Catholic. There was a very rich heritage of traditional devotions to the Blessed Virgin, the local saints and local shrines associated with these. The Church had suffered in the French Revolution and these decades were a time of restoration and renewal. In Lourdes at this time, there was the parish priest, three curates and a chaplain in the hospice, which was run by a community of Sisters. The Sisters were a presence in education and medicine. A community of religious Brothers kept a school for the boys.

The cultivation of corn was a basic in the life of the area. This, in turn, led to the important standing of small flour mills in the economy. The people who owned or lived and worked in these mills were Bernadette's people. For over sixty years before her time they had worked in the Boly Mill and were hopeful of one day buying it out. They were not the poorest of the poor, but that changed in the 1850s for a variety of reasons, and by the time of the apparitions they were lodged in dreadfully poor conditions.

Bernadette's Family

WHEN YOU ARRIVE IN LOURDES TODAY, YOUR EYE IS very quickly drawn to the castle on the hill. In 1844, the town was at the east side of the castle and everything to the west was open countryside dotted with houses and lodgings. The River Gave more or less separated the area in two. There was only one bridge. The mountains supplied plenty of water to work the mills. One canal flowed down by the side of the castle and worked four mills. One of these was the Boly Mill where Bernadette's family lived.

The Boly Mill today strikes one as being rather spacious and solid, in contrast to the contemporaneous Irish famine houses. Life was fairly stable for the tenants until the man of the house, Justin Castérot, Bernadette's maternal grandfather, was killed in a road accident. His young widow, Claire, was left with five children, a boy of ten years, and four older girls, the eldest being Bernarde, who was nineteen years old. It was decided that a husband needed to be found for the eldest daughter, one who, from a practical viewpoint, could work the mill, thus ensuring they remained operating.

A single man aged thirty-four, François Soubirous, appeared on the scene. He was pleasant and hard-working, and work at the Boly Mill continued. However, it soon became apparent that he was not in fact interested in marrying the eldest Bernarde, but rather the second eldest, Louise. Rather than argue his case on emotional grounds, he very practically stated that Louise was the better housekeeper! It was explained to him that the custom was to marry the eldest off first, the 'heir'. At this he simply smiled and continued to work at the mill.

It seems that he proved himself such a capable worker and pleasant man that eventually he got his way. On 9 January 1843, François Soubirous and Louise Castérot were married in the parish church by the parish priest.

A year later, on 7 January 1844, their first child was born. The new baby was baptised Bernarde-Marie, after her aunt Bernarde, but was called Bernadette by all. There were nine children in Bernadette's family, of whom only four survived, the last dying without a birth certificate.[3]

The eldest, whether male or female, had the title of heir, and this was important in the local culture. Growing up, Bernadette was very conscious of her position and responsibilities as the eldest in her family.

When Bernadette was a few months old, her mother had an accident which resulted in her not being able to nurse the baby any more. Four kilometres out of town, in the village of Bartrès, an older female cousin of the family had lost her own baby, so little Bernadette was given to her to nurse. One of the remarkable aspects of that period was the affection shown by Bernadette's father to his little child. At any or no excuse, he was in Bartrès to see her. After some months Bernadette was brought back to her family. For a few years the three generations continued to live in the one house. These were peaceful years for Bernadette.

Then there came a few bad harvests and farmers were struggling. Even if they were bad at paying, François generally felt for them and gave them credit. Both Louise and François were generous with hard-up customers. Then disaster struck again: François lost his left eye in

---

3. Harris, *Lourdes: Body and Spirit in the Secular Age*, 2000, p. 159.

an accident. In the deteriorating economic situation, the family were no longer able to pay the rent, not to mind think of buying out the mill. They had to leave their home in 1854. So began four years of misery and insecurity regarding finding a place to stay and earning some income.

In 1855 there was an outbreak of cholera in Lourdes. Bernadette, who was eleven years of age, escaped the disease. However, having never been of robust health, she now developed very serious asthma. Her attendance at school suffered not only because of her health but also because she needed to avail of any work she could get in order to help feed the family. While Louise, her mother, did some housekeeping, washing and work in the fields, Bernadette looked after her little brother, Justin.

With her failing health it was decided she would be better off out in the fresh air, so she returned to her cousin in Bartrès to work as a shepherd. She liked the work and the companionship of the other girls in the neighbouring fields. Again her father kept close contact. He felt the fresh air was good for her. However, her relationship with the cousin was not good. She was rather cold and lacking in understanding for Bernadette. Part of the arrangement with this woman was that Bernadette would be taught her catechism to prepare her for her First Communion, but she only thought it necessary for Bernadette to learn the catechism answers off by heart in French. It was a lost cause, and she told Bernadette she was stupid and ignorant. Following this, when the parish priest of Bartrès was moved and not replaced, Bernadette decided to take the situation into her own hands. She arrived back mid-week to her family saying that she had to return to Lourdes to make her First Communion, as it was never going to happen in Bartrès.

Meanwhile, things had gone from bad to worse for the family. They decided to seek refuge in a small room owned by a cousin, which had been used as a town jail but had become so foul even for that purpose that it was abandoned altogether. When they asked this cousin if they could stay there, he was horrified at the idea. Later in the day, however, he had second thoughts, and took pity on them. This room, known as the Cachot, looks very different now. Then it was a dark, unwholesome place, with a dung heap outside the window. When the walls grew damp it proved disastrous for Bernadette's asthma.

An incident took place that winter which provides an extraordinary backdrop to what was to come. Four sacks of flour were stolen in Lourdes. The owner went to the police and accused Bernadette's father, who had previously worked for him. François Soubirous was arrested, held in prison and brought to court. At the court he was released because the only evidence against him was that the owner of the flour thought he was so poor that he must have stolen the flour.

The First Apparition

ON THE MORNING OF 11 FEBRUARY 1858, THE THURSDAY before Ash Wednesday, François had no work, and not feeling well remained in bed. Louise could see they were short of sticks for the fire. She asked the second daughter, baptised Marie but called Toinette, to go out and collect some. Toinette and her friend, Jeanne Abadie, called Baloum, went, and Bernadette pleaded to be allowed go too. When she promised to wear her stockings and to wrap herself up well against the damp cold, she was allowed go with them. At around eleven o'clock, they left the Cachot and were soon on their way out of town heading towards the old bridge. At the bridge an elderly woman suggested that they go down to the Old Rock, Massabielle, near where the canal meets the River Gave, as some trees had recently been cut down in the area.[4] They followed her advice and soon they were standing opposite the Massabielle between the little canal stream and the fast-flowing river. When people at the scene today try to imagine what happened next, they often get confused as the canal that flowed in front of Massabielle is now all covered over and the river has been pushed back.

On reaching the canal, Bernadette's companions decided to search for firewood on the other side. They took off their timber clogs, ran across the stream – complaining about the cold water – and they were away. Bernadette asked them to wait for her while she removed her shoes and stockings, but they ignored her. As she bent down to remove her first stocking she heard a little gust of wind. On looking up she saw nothing, but when she proceeded to remove the second stocking she heard the sound of the wind again. A gentle light was gradually brightening the darkness in the niche at the side of the rock. She recognised a smile and then a beautiful girl in white, with hands stretched out in a gesture of welcome. Bernadette rubbed her eyes hard a few times. When she opened them again the smiling girl in white was still there. Bernadette herself recalled:

---

4. René Laurentin, *Bernadette of Lourdes*, London: Darton, Longman & Todd, 1979, p. 34.

I put my hand in my pocket, and I found my rosary there. I wanted to make the Sign of the Cross. I couldn't raise my hand to my forehead. It collapsed on me. My hand was trembling. The vision made the Sign of the Cross. Then I tried a second time, and I was able. As soon as I made the Sign of the Cross, the shock of fear I felt disappeared. I knelt down and I said my rosary in the presence of the beautiful lady. The vision fingered the beads of her own rosary but she did not move her lips. When I finished my rosary, she signed for me to approach; but I did not dare. Then she disappeared, just like that.[5]

Then it was back to the drizzle and the grey rocks. Bernadette had already removed one stocking. She now took off the second one and happily crossed the stream, wondering why the other girls were complaining about the cold. She was in good spirits and sat on a stone as she put her stockings and shoes back on. The others had seen her on her knees praying at the grotto, prompting Baloum to comment: 'It is stupid to pray there. It is definitely enough to pray in the church!'[6]

Her companions returned with a good supply of firewood. They took shelter under the roof of the grotto and began to dance around to warm themselves. Bernadette became annoyed, and asked them, 'Did you see anything?' They were curious now and asked her what she had seen. She tried to change the topic. 'You were joking when you told me the water was cold. I thought it

---

5. Ibid., p. 41.

6. Ibid., p. 34.

was warm,' she said, as she tried to carry out an inspection of the grotto. At this stage, Baloum had had enough and said, 'She hasn't seen anything at all. She just didn't want to gather any sticks. Her mother will give her a good scolding.' She then set off home, leaving the two sisters alone. Bernadette took her share of the sticks, and headed up the steep climb to the road, getting there before her very surprised sister, who always saw herself as the healthier and stronger one.[7] Toinette was becoming more and more intrigued and pleaded with her sister to share what she had seen, promising not to tell anyone, not even their mother. So Bernadette told her younger sister what she had seen, leaving Toinette somewhat frightened by what she heard. She was also always somewhat jealous of Bernadette, the eldest, who had stockings because of her asthma, and white bread for her stomach.

When they got back to their one-room lodging, their mother set about cleaning the girls' hair, being terrified of the threat of skin infection. She started with Toinette, who was annoyed watching Bernadette already eating her bread. Toinette described what happened next: 'Something was driving me to tell what Bernadette had said to me. So three times I went "hmm", as if I was trying to clear my throat. My mother said: "Why are you doing that? Are you sick?" "No," I said, "but I was going to tell you what Bernadette told me."'

Then Toinette blurted out: 'Bernadette saw a white girl in the grotto of Massabielle.' Her mother turned to Bernadette, and asked her what she saw. 'Something white' was the answer. This was too much for the mother:

---

7. Ibid., p. 35.

what with moving to an old jail cell, with all the struggles, with François's term in prison, and now this! Soon she was hopping the stick for beating the bedclothes off the two girls, telling them, 'You didn't see anything but a white rock. I forbid you to go back there.'[8]

That evening, as the family said their usual prayers, Bernadette was experiencing a deep peace, and tears began to flow. As soon as she could, her mother discussed her troubles with her neighbour.

The next day, Friday, Bernadette wanted to go back to the grotto but her mother told her to do her work. On Saturday evening, the chaplain in the hospice and a teacher in the First Communion class for the poor children, Fr Pomian, was hearing confessions as usual. Then this young girl said through the grill: 'I saw something white in the shape of a lady.' He let her talk and was astonished at how coherent her story was. When she mentioned 'the gust of wind', he immediately thought of the gust in the story of the descent of the Holy Spirit on the first believers at Pentecost. He was surprised at the story but did not think it amounted to much. Still he did ask Bernadette if he could speak to the parish priest, Dean Peyramale, about it. Bernadette agreed, and indeed was rather surprised at the deference shown her. That evening, the curate and parish priest discussed the matter briefly, and passed on to other matters with, 'We must wait and see'.

Meanwhile, Bernadette was being told by her mother and her mother's friend that she had dreamt up the events.[9] Her mother couldn't help wondering if it was

---

8. Ibid., p. 37.

9. Ibid.

'the soul of one of our relations in purgatory', or even if it was an evil spirit.[10]

The next move seems to have come from Toinette, Baloum, and their pals, who all wanted to see what Bernadette saw. After Mass on Sunday, 14 February, they decided to go and get permission from her mother for Bernadette to go to the grotto. She refused at first, but eventually sent them off to ask Bernadette's father, François, for permission. They found him working with the man who ran the local stagecoach line. François at first refused, but his employer took the side of the girls, saying that a lady with a rosary can't be bad. François gave in but warned them to be back for Vespers, as it was Sunday.

They went to the parish church first to take some holy water with them as a defence against any evil spirit. With Bernadette they headed for the grotto, descending the steep slope from the Forest Road. To their amazement, sickly Bernadette got there first and they found her already on her knees, saying the rosary. At the second decade Bernadette's face changed, and she said out loud: 'There she is.' But the others saw nothing. Bernadette began sprinkling the holy water in the direction of the apparition, demanding her to 'stay if [she] came from God, or go away if not'. 'But the more I sprinkled, the more she smiled; and I kept sprinkling until the bottle was empty.' Bernadette had grown pale but she was very happy and radiated peace. Still there was a lot of anxiety among the others. Baloum, who had remained on the slope above the grotto, sent a stone tumbling down

10. René Laurentin, *Lourdes: Histoire Authentique des Apparitions*, Vol. 2, Paris: P. Lethielleux, 1961, pp. 190–1.

the side, landing near Bernadette. Some of the young people ran away shouting. Braver ones wanted to help Bernadette, but she seemed oblivious to everything and they found her too heavy to move. They enlisted the help of a miller from nearby, a strong man used to handling heavy sacks. She was so small but so heavy, and the miller got her to the mill with great difficulty.

At this point, rumours were beginning to circulate among the people of the town. When Bernadette turned up for catechism class on Monday morning at the school for poor girls, preparing as she was for First Communion, she was already the focus of fun and derision. People regarded the grotto as a pig shelter, and Bernadette was being teased about the girl with bare feet. One of the Sisters asked her: 'Have you finished with your carnival extravaganzas?' [11]

An Interested Parishioner

ON SHROVE TUESDAY, 16 FEBRUARY, THE CURIOSITY OF a rather well-off woman, Madame Milhet, was aroused. She had heard the story from her seamstress, Antoinette Peyret, the bailiff's daughter who had employed Louise Soubirous a number of times. On Ash Wednesday evening, she went to the old prison and said she would take Bernadette to the grotto in the morning. At 5 a.m. the next day, 18 February, she and Antoinette collected Bernadette, and all three attended the first Mass of the day. Antoinette was carrying her father's pen and inkstand with her as they went to the grotto. They had

---

11. Laurentin, *Bernadette of Lourdes*, 1979, p. 41.

decided that the lady should write down her name. Again Bernadette was first at the grotto. As soon as they started the rosary Bernadette announced: 'She is here!' Antoinette handed Bernadette the inkstand. They saw Bernadette smiling as she asked the lady to write her name. The onlookers heard nothing. When they quizzed Bernadette about not asking, she told them that she did ask and the lady, beginning to laugh, had told her: 'It is not necessary.' While Bernadette herself had laughed at this answer, the two women were annoyed.

However the girl in white had her own request: 'Would you graciously come here for the next fortnight?' Bernadette was surprised to be spoken to so courteously and was struck by the soft and delicate voice. She immediately promised that she would. Then, in Bernadette's words, 'She told me also that she did not promise to make me happy in this world, but in the other.' This meeting was a whole new experience for Bernadette. She reported that: 'She looked on me as one person talking to another.' She, who so often had been made to feel bad about herself, was full of peace.

On the way back to the town, Madame Milhet decided to take charge of things. She arranged for Bernadette to stay in her house. That way she could accompany her to the grotto in secret, without all the coming and going between the two houses. But now Louise wanted to go along and so did Bernarde, Bernadette's aunt. Word was spreading.

On Friday, 19 February, the day of the fourth apparition and the first day of the fortnight that Bernadette had been asked so courteously by the vision to come to the grotto, eight people were present. Next day, there were thirty, and on Sunday, 21 February, there were a hundred.

The apparition was staying silent, but the fervour of those praying the rosary at the grotto was growing intense. They shared Bernadette's joy though she was the only one who saw anything. The big question was: who is it? This new presence was now not only causing a stir in Bernadette's family but in the wider parish.

When Bernadette came out of Sunday school on 21 February, the day of the sixth apparition, the Police Commissioner Jacomet was waiting for her and brought her to the house where he was staying. A crowd gathered but he would not allow any of them in, not even any of her family. One of the men staying with him in the house, Jean-Baptiste Estrade, a tax collector, was a discreet witness.

Jacomet began with asking Bernadette her personal details, her name, age, family.

'Can you read and write?'

'No, sir.'

'Have you made your First Communion?'

'No, sir.'

The interview took place in the local language though the policeman took his notes in French. He was relaxed at first. He decided that Bernadette was simple and sincere. So his thoughts turned to who was behind her? Who was making her go to the grotto? Who had given her the idea that she had seen the Holy Virgin?

'So then, Bernadette, did you see the Holy Virgin?'

'I did not say I have seen the Holy Virgin.'

'Ah, good! You haven't seen anything!'

'Yes, I did see something.'

'Well, what did you see?'

'Something white.'

'Some thing or some one?'

'That thing [*aquerò*] has the form of a young girl [*damisèle*].'

'You say *aquerò*, that thing … And that thing did not say to you: "I am the Holy Virgin"?'

'*Aquerò* did not say that to me.'

'But that is what people in the town are saying.'

'Yes, that is what people were saying and the local paper was saying so mockingly!'

'Well, then, this young lady – how was she dressed?'

'A white dress, tied with a blue ribbon, a white veil on her head, and a yellow rose on each foot … the colour of the chain of her rosary …'

'She had feet?'

'Her dress and the roses hid them, except for her toes.'

'She was pretty?'

'Oh yes, sir, very beautiful.'

The policeman also took down the details of people involved with Bernadette. His focus remained on finding out who was telling her what she should say, why she was doing what she did, and how to put an end to the whole thing.

'Listen, Bernadette, everyone is laughing at you. They say you are mad. For your own sake, you must not go back to the grotto anymore!'

'I promised to go for fifteen days.'[12]

---

12. Ibid., p. 51.

New Things are Happening

BERNADETTE FELT DRAWN TO THE GROTTO AND WAS determined to keep the promise she had made. The comments of the police did not have much effect; on Monday, 22 February, she was back, accompanied by fifty women and two gendarmes.[13] This turned out to be one of the two days of the fortnight when the vision did not appear. But on the following day she had her seventh apparition.

Her experience at the grotto was an experience of being recognised and treated with courtesy by this young lady. She was finding a new inner strength that enabled her to withstand the often hurtful comments of the other children and adults. One of the things that caused the most amazement for those who were with her at any of the apparitions (where they themselves saw nothing) was the transformation in Bernadette. So many spoke of the beauty of her face. For Bernadette, the grotto was becoming an experience of prayer and a friendship full of peace and beauty. At her second interrogation, this time by Prosecutor Dutour, she said: 'I feel so much joy when I go there.'[14] For those with her it was becoming an experience of prayer, peace, beauty and togetherness.

Her parents, however, were finding the whole thing very trying. They had already suffered so much in the eyes of the public. They had had enough of vexing matters and ridicule. Now they wanted to be left alone. Instead, though, they found themselves being carried along by events. They were often annoyed by Bernadette, but they were also loyal and protective. Bernadette's extended

13. Harris, *Lourdes: Body and Spirit in the Secular Age*, 2000, p. 6.
14. Laurentin, *Bernadette of Lourdes*, 1979, p. 62.

family was being drawn into things as well. They were unsure of what was happening and they often struggled to be supportive.

The police were perplexed by all the excitement and felt that it was a threat to public order. Still, they did not have much to object to. The people going to the grotto did so quietly; Bernadette was only a child; and there was growing support for her. But there was also a certain amount of comment that this was the nineteenth century and that superstition and that kind of irrationality belonged to the past. The whole thing was felt by some to be an embarrassment.

The clergy were keeping out of it, while trying to stay informed. Father Pomian seems to have been quite friendly with Bernadette and at one point told her that no one could stop her going to the grotto. Dean Peyramale had forbidden the other priests to go near the grotto. He himself was in contact with Jean-Baptiste Estrade, the discreet witness at the first police interrogation who was convinced of Bernadette's sincerity early on and who attended the apparitions. Some of the religious Sisters in the town took an opposing view and were quite hard on Bernadette and her reports.

In all the excitement, people were taking very different attitudes. Many in immediate contact with Bernadette believed that something new was happening in their parish. Many were becoming more aware of their faith, and some were talking about the Virgin Mary appearing to Bernadette. It is interesting to note that Bernadette never named the vision except to call her the 'beautiful girl' or *aquerò*. At the other end there were the people who felt they knew, without any investigation, that this could not be happening. This was the nineteenth century after all! Still, everybody wanted some story or some explanation to help them relate to events.

From this stage on, a mass of note-taking began to take place around the events so that today we have a great deal of documentation.

The Apparitions Continue

ON WEDNESDAY, 24 FEBRUARY, FOR THE EIGHTH apparition, the crowd numbered 250. It was no longer just the poor who came. Educated and better-off people were joining in and being touched by the experience. This was now the second week of Lent. Bernadette announced that the vision had used a new word that day – 'Penance'. The crowd had seen her in ecstasy as she said her rosary. Next there seemed to follow the same atmosphere of smiles and friendly laughter as before, except this gentle atmosphere was now sometimes coloured with sadness and tears. People saw her advance a couple of paces on her knees before seeming to throw herself on the ground. Afterwards she explained that the vision spoke of penance and asked for prayers for the conversion of sinners. She asked her to perform an act of penance: 'Go and kiss the ground as a penance for sinners.' Bernadette never forgot how the sadness of the beautiful girl conveyed the sadness of sin.

That day, a teacher who was alongside her during the apparition asked Bernadette if the apparition spoke. Bernadette was amazed that she had not heard for herself, as Bernadette presumed everybody else could hear too. Then the teacher asked did the apparition speak

French or patois, to which Bernadette, again in surprise, replied: 'Speak French to me? Sure I do not know any! She spoke in patois and used *bous'* – '*bous'* being the patois for the polite form of the French for 'you'. The teacher was fascinated by the respect this beautiful girl had for Bernadette, and maybe also fascinated by how much it meant to Bernadette to be so respected.

The next day, 25 February, the crowd had increased to three hundred. From the beginning of the apparition, Bernadette began crawling on her knees. People heard her repeating the word 'penance – penance – penance', as if she was repeating what was being said to her. She moved towards the River Gave but turned again and went back towards the grotto, now walking upright. She then bent down and began to dig with her hands at a muddy patch of ground. It was all very new for the onlookers as they had become used to the serenity and beauty of the scene. Now they saw Bernadette putting the wet mud to her mouth, rubbing her face with it and picking some grass and eating it. People were really shocked, though they were amazed at the agility of this sick child. Bernadette's own account of the apparition says:

Aquerò told me to go and drink at the well and wash myself. Seeing no well I went to drink at the stream. She said it was not there: she pointed with her finger that I was to go under the rock. I went and I found a puddle of water that was more like mud, and there was so little of it that I could hardly get any into my hands. Nevertheless I obeyed, and I started scratching the ground: after doing that I was able to take some. The water was so dirty that three times I threw it away: the fourth time I was able to drink it. She made me eat grass growing in the same place where I had drunk: once only; I don't know why. Then the Vision disappeared and I went home.[15]

So many people had come to the grotto because of the accounts of the beauty of Bernadette's face during the apparitions. Now they felt the whole scene was just ugly. By way of explanation for her behaviour, all they got from Bernadette was: 'For sinners.'

The crowd dispersed that morning rather subdued. However, some individuals returned to the spot later in the day and found water spouting out of the ground and becoming clearer all the time. Some people may even have taken water away that day.

The headmaster of the high school in Lourdes, Antoine Clarens, set about preparing a memorandum for the prefect of the district. He knew that recent events at the grotto had caused some upset and he questioned Bernadette on these. She explained the meaning of her strange actions: 'In penance, first for myself, and then for others.' In her answers he only found objectivity, even 'indifference', with a naturalness, assurance, naivety and charm that disarmed him. After the interview it seems Clarens was the one who was less sure of himself.[16]

By Sunday, 28 February, the crowd had increased to 1,500 people, wedged in between the sheer cliff and the River Gave. The commandant of the constabulary forces

---

15. André Ravier, *Bernadette: The Saint of Poverty and of Light*, Paris: Nouvelle Librairie de France, 1974, p. 17.

16. René Laurentin, *Bernadette Vous Parle*, Tome 1, Lourdes: Oeuvre de la Grotte, 1972, p. 93.

in Tarbes felt he had to review the situation. Bernadette was continuing with her penitential exercises. Then on Monday, 1 March, a priest who was not from Lourdes, and was unaware that Dean Peyramale had forbidden the clergy to go to the grotto, arrived and caused a bit of a sensation. He was surprised to find people making sure he got a place right alongside Bernadette. He saw her in ecstasy:

> Her smile passes all description. Neither the most capable artist nor the most consummate actor could ever reproduce her charm and grace. It is impossible to imagine it. What struck me was the joy and the sadness on her face. When one succeeded the other, it happened with the speed of lightning. But ... there was nothing brusque about it: a marvellous transition. I had observed the child when she came to the grotto. I had watched her with meticulous attention. What a difference there was between the girl she was then and the girl I saw at the moment of the apparition! Respect, silence, recollection reigned everywhere. Oh, how good it was there! I thought I was in the vestibule of paradise.[17]

That day, one of the first of seven cures that would eventually be regarded by the bishop of Tarbes, Monsignor Laurence, as being the 'work of God', took place. A woman with a paralysis in the hand had plunged it into the water of the spring and it suddenly regained its suppleness. Subsequently, the sick, and those who

---

17. Laurentin, *Bernadette of Lourdes*, 1979, pp. 65–6.

cared for them, turned up in ever-greater numbers to the grotto and the well.

In July 1858, a few weeks after the final apparition, Mgr Laurence set up an Episcopal Commission of Inquiry. They spent a lot of time investigating the cures. They sifted through the substantial documentation. They then focused on twenty-nine cases. They finally accepted six, all happening between 1 March 1858 and 9 November 1858. One was that of a very sick two-year-old, Justin Bouhorts, who came from a very poor family. As her last hope, the child's mother plunged him into the water at Lourdes. That night he slept peacefully, and from then on enjoyed good health. Louis Bouriette, a fifty-year-old quarryman, who was in danger of losing the sight in his right eye because of a twenty-year-old injury, was cured in March 1858. Henri Busquet, about fifteen years of age, had a recurring tumour in the glands of his neck, but was cured of his affliction on 28 April 1858. Blaisette Cazenave was fifty years of age when she was cured of a chronic infection of the conjunctiva and the eyelids in March 1858. Madeleine Rizan de Nay was around fifty-eight years when she received Lourdes water from a friend. For about twenty years she had been wasting away with sickness and had great difficulty in eating. She drank the water and washed herself in it, and was cured. Marie Moreau was a seventeen-year-old girl who for ten months experienced deteriorating sight, being in danger of losing the sight in one eye altogether. She was cured on 9 November 1858.

The Call to Witness

ON TUESDAY, 2 MARCH, THERE WAS ANOTHER development. This time *aquerò* had a new message: 'Go and tell the priests that people are to come here in procession and to build a chapel here.' Bernadette turned to her family to help her carry out this commission. Supported by two aunts she arrived at the presbytery. From the start, Dean Peyramale was on edge.

'You're the one who goes to the grotto?'

'Yes, Reverend Father.'

'And you say that you see the Holy Virgin?'

'I did not say it is the Holy Virgin.'

'Then who is this lady?'

'I don't know.'

'So you don't know! Liar! Yet those you get to run after you and the newspaper say you claim to see the Holy Virgin. Well, then, what do you see?'

'Something that resembles a lady.'[18]

At this stage it is good to remember that both Bernadette and Dean Peyramale were part of a parish where many other people felt involved in all that was going on. This was a community event. Even if Bernadette was careful not to speculate about the identity of *aquerò*, many others were definite that it was the Holy Virgin. They were also wondering out loud about something big that would happen on the Thursday when the fortnight would end. When they heard that the lady had given Bernadette a message to 'go and tell the priests that the people are to come here in procession and to build a chapel here', some went immediately to the parish priest

---

18. Ibid., p. 68.

and told him that the Virgin wanted a procession on the last day of the fortnight. The dean knew the civil authorities would be rather unhappy about a procession, and that the bishop would not be very enthusiastic either.

It is also helpful at this point to consider the wider Church context at this time. Pope Pius IX had just declared a special jubilee of prayer, and every bishop was to choose the most suitable time for devotions in his diocese. The Bishop of Tarbes asked the senior priest in each deanery (a local grouping of parishes) to arrange for a special preacher to visit the parishes during two weeks of Lent. Dean Peyramale was charged with this responsibility in the Lourdes area, but he was unable to find anyone suitable.

So while Dean Peyramale was concerned about the events with Bernadette and the apparitions, he couldn't help but be impressed by the change for the better in many parishioners. There were more people coming to confession and attending Mass with more devotion. People were doing penance and turning to the practice of the faith with more devotion. And while Dean Peyramale had failed in his quest to find a suitable preacher, Lent, it seemed, was happening all the same – and a very successful one at that!

Before long, however, the dean grew tired of the whole event and dismissed Bernadette and her aunts. In the confusion, they had left the presbytery before Bernadette realised that while she had conveyed the request for the procession, she had forgotten about the chapel. Her aunts were not keen on going back. Dominiquette Cazenave, a former employer of her father, arranged for another meeting later that evening. This time there were several priests at the meeting.

Accompanied by Dominiquette, Bernadette reported that she was told to tell the priests to have a chapel built.

'You still don't know what her name is?'

'No, Reverend Father.'

'Well, then, you must ask her.'[19]

Bernadette left the meeting on Dominiquette's arm, feeling buoyant. 'I am quite content. I did what I was asked to do.'

While not everybody was putting Bernadette on a pedestal, she had enough support to carry on doing what she felt she was asked to do. She had her place in the parish.

The Last Day of the Fortnight

THURSDAY, 4 MARCH ARRIVED AND THERE WAS A LOT of talk that this would be a 'big day'. The previous evening, Police Commissioner Jacomet had visited the grotto and inspected all the cavities to make sure there was no machinery or fireworks planted there to ensure a 'miracle'. He was astonished to find people there already. And they were praying! He repeated his inspection at 5 a.m. on the morning of 4 March. Estimates of the crowd varied from 8,000 to 20,000, with a large crowd occupying the land at the far side of the River Gave. Police from neighbouring stations had to be brought in and the soldiers from the castle were on hand. There was continuous prayer and great calm in rather difficult conditions.

---

19. Ibid., p. 69.

When Bernadette arrived she was accompanied by a grown-up cousin – a school teacher named Jeanne Védère. The two had attended 6.30 a.m. Mass. The crowd made way for Bernadette but her cousin was separated from her. On arriving at her place, Bernadette asked that her cousin be allowed pass to be with her. The police found her and brought her forward to Bernadette's side. There was a growing respect for Bernadette.

In his well-documented account, René Laurentin writes:

At the third Hail Mary of the second decade of the rosary, Bernadette's appearance changed. The police commissioner Jacomet and the deputy mayor were busy taking notes in their books. Jacomet was particularly diligent in noting every gesture that Bernadette made: 'Thirty-four smiles and twenty-four bows in the direction of the grotto.' The crowd imitated her Signs of the Cross. After a half hour, Bernadette went under the roof of the grotto to the place where she held her conversations with the apparition. Her lips moved, but no sound filtered out to the crowd around her. For two minutes she remained there, completely happy. During those two minutes alone, according to Jeanne Védère, Bernadette smiled eighteen times, grew sad sometimes, then brightened up again.[20]

The apparition had been a long one, lasting a good three-quarters of an hour (from 7:15 to 8 a.m.). Laurentin continues his account by saying that the crowd was calm

---
20. Ibid., 73.

but perplexed. The police were feeling triumphant – public order had been maintained without incident or accident. They were also pleased that the expectation from some of the crowd of something spectacular happening had been disappointed, something indeed that the press had a great discussion about.

Now the people began to constantly call to the miserable room in which Bernadette and her family lived, to touch her, embrace her. Bernadette was not at all happy with this. When she was asked to bless a rosary beads, she protested: 'I am not a priest.' During a lull that day she managed to visit Dean Peyramale, who queried:

'What did the lady say?'

'I asked her for her name … she smiled. I asked her to make the rose-bush flower, she kept smiling. But she still wants the chapel.'

'Do you have the money to build this chapel?'

'No, Reverend Father.'

'Neither do I. Tell the lady to give it to you.'[21]

Now people wanted to give Bernadette money and gifts. Again this upset her badly. 'Nobody could get the little girl to accept even the smallest sum of money, even for her parents.'[22] The police had organised people to offer her money. She rejected everything firmly.

In the days that followed the fortnight of apparitions, the crowds continued to frequent the grotto. More and more candles were being left there. There was more talk of cures but nothing decisive. The editorial of the local paper was very sure of itself:

---

21. Ibid., p. 75.

22. Laurentin, *Bernadette Vous Parle,* Tome 1, 1972, p. 166.

What a disappointment! … How these poor credulous people have been humiliated … How many of them have realised, all too late unfortunately, the ridiculousness of the behaviour and regretted their excessive credulity![23]

Other papers joined in with the same confidence.

'I am the Immaculate Conception'

VERY EARLY ON THE MORNING OF 25 MARCH, THE Feast of the Annunciation, Bernadette woke up with a new urge to go to the grotto. Her parents wanted to stop her but in the end they asked her to wait. By 5 a.m. she was on her way. Though there had been a three-week lull and no previous indication from Bernadette, there were about one hundred people waiting at the grotto. Some of them were very aware of the feast day and expected something to happen on that day.

This time Bernadette was determined to get an answer for Dean Peyramale regarding the identity of the lady. After the rosary she was delighted when *aquerò* approached her. She had been preparing for three weeks now for this moment. As solemnly as she could, she said in the local language: 'Mademoiselle, would you be so kind as to tell me who you are, if you please?'

Aquerò smiled. She did not reply. Bernadette repeated the question insistently a second and third time. *Aquerò* smiled all the while. This time, however, Bernadette would not let her alone, because an answer was the

---

23. Ibid., p. 117.

precondition laid down by the dean for the building of a chapel.

A fourth time Bernadette asked the question. *Aquerò* stopped 'laughing'. She joined her hands, opened them out and extended them towards the ground. Then she joined them again around her bosom, raised her eyes to the sky, and said: '*Que soy era Immaculada Councepciou.*'[24] I am the Immaculate Conception.

Bernadette set off immediately to find Dean Peyramale. To make sure she did not forget the words she kept repeating them as she ran, refusing to answer any questions from anyone. She got to the parish priest and blurted out: 'I am the Immaculate Conception.'

Dean Peyramale was on edge and seems to have been on the point of saying: 'Who do you think you are?' Bernadette recognised what was happening and said: 'The lady said "I am the Immaculate Conception".'

'A woman cannot have that name! You are mistaken! Do you know what that means?'

Bernadette shook her head: 'No.'

'Then how can you say the words if you do not understand them?'

'I kept repeating them along the way.'

Peyramale was lost for words this time.

Bernadette added: 'She still wants the chapel.'

'Go back home. I will see you another day.'[25]

The parish priest did not know what to make of it all. He sat down and wrote a letter to the bishop. He felt he had done his duty.

---

24. Laurentin, *Bernadette of Lourdes*, 1979, pp. 81–2.
25. Ibid., p. 82.

Bernadette had no notion of what the phrase meant. Later that day somebody explained it to her. Now at last she could say who it was – the Blessed Virgin Mary. Now she could relax in the joy of it all.

Bernadette returned to school to prepare for her First Communion. On 27 March, three doctors, acting on the orders of the prefect, examined Bernadette. They were in a difficult position as they knew that the prefect was waiting for them to give a certificate committing Bernadette to hospital, but they found nothing to justify such a decision. Afterwards Bernadette said: 'They wanted me to believe that I am sick, but I am not sick at all', and at this she laughed.[26]

Then on 7 April, Easter Wednesday, Bernadette went to the grotto again and saw the apparition. A medical doctor, Dr Dozous, who previously had been highly critical of Bernadette and her visions, declared: 'Now I believe', and reported that 'as a scientific observer' he wanted to state that he saw the flame of Bernadette's candle lick the palms of her hands for several minutes without leaving a single trace of any burning on the skin.[27]

After this there was a period of calm for Bernadette. Some protective friends took her to Cauterets and its medicinal waters for her asthma. However, the fervour in the area continued, and the civil authorities grew increasingly annoyed with all the excitement. They decided that the trouble was the grotto. People were gathering regularly to pray, sing hymns and hold processions. The stream of water was channelled to make it more readily available, a platform for the candles

---

26. Ravier, *Bernadette*, 1974, p. 24.

27. Laurentin, *Bernadette of Lourdes*, 1979, p. 85.

was built, and the sharp descent behind the grotto was improved and made safer. One of the police witnesses who regarded these people as normally only interested in getting something for themselves was now witness to all kinds of gifts being left at the grotto, even money and then a gold coin. When he asked one poor woman for an explanation he was told: 'It's for the Virgin.'

After the vision had identified herself on the Feast of the Annunciation as the Immaculate Conception, people felt a new confidence. They had already placed an altar in the grotto with a statue and a light on it. Now carpenters built railings to protect it. The authorities felt they had to act. No permission had been obtained to build an oratory in this public place. Baron Oscar Massy was the prefect for the department and its highest civil authority. The department was the unit of civil administration that joined the central state in Paris to the local authorities. The local police commissioner, Jacomet, had been keeping Massy informed of every detail of events in Lourdes. He, in turn, was reporting to the Ministry of the Interior in Paris. Massy, a religious man, was determined not only to preserve religion from superstition, but also to maintain the proper order. On 4 May, orders were given by Massy to remove all the pious objects such as statues, pictures and candles from the grotto. Police Commissioner Jacomet had difficulty in finding somebody with a horse and cart who was prepared to remove all that had been brought to decorate the grotto. Eventually he did, but the unfortunate owner of the cart found himself being told that he would not have any luck for his efforts. The people were appalled by this profanation of a sacred space that had become so precious to them.

On 25 May, Bernadette returned from Cauterets where she had been closely observed by the police.[28] They found nothing to object to in her behaviour. The authorities were now ever more inclined to look to the grotto as the problem, as Bernadette was very respectful of the civil authorities. On 3 June 1858, the feast of Corpus Christi, she made her First Communion. On 13 June, the grotto was declared out of bounds. The local people were very angry. Barricades were erected on 15 June, but demolished on 17 June; erected again on 18 June and demolished again on the night of 27 June. They were erected again on 28 June, demolished on the night of 4 July, and erected again on 10 July. Sometimes it was the same people who erected them during the day that demolished them at night. Some people were prepared to do a paid day's work for the police, but had more local loyalties at night. The police desperately tried to dissuade the crowds, taking down names and addresses. On 11 July, the Bishop of Tarbes asked for restraint and calm was restored.

On the evening of 16 July, Bernadette felt drawn to the grotto for what was to be the last of the apparitions. She tried her best not to attract any attention. This time she went in the opposite direction to her usual route. She made her way to the meadow on the opposite side of the River Gave. René Laurentin describes what happened next:

Groups of people were there on their knees, praying silently in the direction of the barricaded grotto across the way. Bernadette knelt down too and lit her

28. Laurentin, *Bernadette Vous Parle*, Tome 1, 1972, p. 154.

candle. It was one flame among many in the gathering darkness. She had come along with her Aunt Lucile. Two other parishioners joined them silently. The rosary was scarcely begun when Bernadette's hands opened wide in a greeting of joyous surprise. Her face went pale and lit up, as it had during the fifteen days of the apparitions. She recited the rosary for a length of time that no one thought to measure. Then she got up. It was over. This final apparition had been a silent one, like the first few. On the way back home she had only this to say: 'I saw neither the boards nor the Gave. It seemed to me that I was in the grotto, no more distant than the other times. I saw only the Holy Virgin.'[29]

A Parish Changing

THE PARISH OF LOURDES WOULD NEVER BE THE SAME again. The first people involved in this transformation were three young girls. For the second apparition there were ten young girls, all from the religion class attended by the poor girls of the parish. Then their families, neighbours, work contacts, school and Church contacts were drawn into events. This involvement of a wide variety of people was central to the founding of the new Lourdes.

The poor were the first to get involved in the prayer at the grotto, especially the women. Among them the sick and the suffering were a very strong presence. They prayed together in faith and hope. While Bernadette insisted that she did not know who the vision was, these people

---

29. Laurentin, *Bernadette of Lourdes*, 1979, p. 90.

prayed the rosary, convinced that the Blessed Virgin was with them. The educated and the better-off were slower to get involved. Perhaps part of their contribution was the enormous record we have today of these events. There are records of all kinds from witnesses, records of interrogations, police and local authority reports, medical reports and clerical reports. We also have letters and personal memoirs.

While the witness of Bernadette remained foundational, the grotto itself very quickly became a source of new life and energy for this Church community. It called some to pray and challenged others. The discovery of the well and the water that flowed from it became a sign of the healing power of God. The call to penance caused people to go to confession, to try and reform their lives and to be more responsible members of the community. The parish priest knew the parish was having a good Lent. The police saw crime decreasing. Since that first gust of wind on 11 February, the Holy Spirit was asking new things of people with which they were not always comfortable. Still, some were finding new hope. Many were being gathered. One account of the crowds says:

Our meadow was covered in people on foot, on horseback, in carts or carriages. It was an impossible sight, really striking. A religious silence prevailed everywhere, the devout contemplation of faith and prayer. At a given signal, everyone, the soldiers on surveillance duty and the civil servants alike, took off their hats, bowed their heads, crossed themselves, and prayed, following Bernadette's example. All ranks of society mingled there: barons, counts, marquises and dukes merged with the crowd of countrymen and workers from the towns.[30]

Amidst the mounting tension in the community between the authorities who wanted to remove the grotto and the locals who wanted it kept, several people, both adults and children, were claiming to have visions. Prefect Massy now announced that anybody who claimed to see a vision would be jailed. A notice was also posted saying that it was forbidden to leave anything at the grotto. The next day, the Children of Mary, 'whose ranks were filled with the pious of good family',[31] after their May devotions in the parish church, walked to the grotto with lighted candles. They said their prayers and then returned with their lighted candles. The first torchlight procession had taken place.

Then the quarry workers, who had already carried out voluntary work around the grotto, announced that for their pattern, or festival, they would go in procession with lighted candles to the shrine. Jacomet appealed to Dean Payramale to restrain them. The quarrymen and their fellow workers acceded to the wishes of the dean and they called off their dance and made the Mass of Ascension Day the focus of their celebration. Between reports of miraculous cures, visionaries, the Children of Mary and quarry workers with their carpenter friends, the patience of the civil authorities was being sorely tested.

Dean Peyramale and the bishop Monsignor Laurence encouraged the people to remain calm. The visions

---

30. Harris, *Lourdes: Body and Spirit in the Secular Age*, 2000, p. 67.

31. Ibid., p. 90

stopped and even the Church authorities were amazed at the restraint of the people. On 22 May, Dr Dozous, who had seen the candle lick the palm of Bernadette without causing any burns, began to take down statements from those who had taken water from the spring and been cured.

On 8 June, it was announced that anybody who went to the grotto would be prosecuted and the local policeman Callet was to take the details of any trespassers. People began to send small children to go through the barriers and leave their candles at the grotto. Then people from very high society in France began to appear and Callet became unsure in his role. Locals welcomed visitors and accompanied them a certain distance towards the grotto. Afterwards, they might invite them to visit the parish church for confession and communion. As time passed, things began to get more ridiculous. Callet had a little dog and when he would decide to visit the grotto he would send the dog off in front so people knew that they should make themselves scarce. Things got more difficult for the civil authorities when, on 28 July 1858, the bishop set up a commission of inquiry. The people of Lourdes knew they were experiencing something special and they were prepared to bear witness to that experience. Their actions were bearing fruit; the cultivation of God's field was continuing. Meanwhile, the story of Lourdes was becoming something of national interest in France.

Leaving Home

BERNADETTE RETURNED AFTER EACH APPARITION TO her family in the Cachot. In September 1858, the

Soubirous family moved to better accommodation. A doctor had told Bernadette's mother that for the sake of the children she must get a better place to stay. People were shocked by the terrible conditions in the Cachot. While Bernadette was very anxious not to use her position for material gain, it was noted that some visitors were embarrassed by the conditions she was living in, and the decision was made to move.

Dean Peyramale had earlier suggested that Bernadette might be able to live with the Sisters who ran the hospice. She told him: 'I understand what you mean, Father; but I love my mother and father so much.'

During and after the apparitions Bernadette was still trying to help earn some money for the family by doing some childminding and housework. At home she felt responsible for the care of the younger children. Because she missed so much schooling, she availed of help with lessons from a generous parishioner. In the middle of all of that, she was answering questions from all sorts of visitors. This might be at home or wherever she was summoned to – the presbytery, the hospice, the Hôtel des Pyrénées or private homes. The curate, Fr Pomian, said she herself was 'the best proof of the apparitions'. René Laurentin sums up her approach as follows:

> It was not only her gift for repartee but also the natural economy of her responses that saved her. She responded directly to the question she was asked, never going further. She was completely indifferent to the effect she produced. She made no effort to convince people, avoiding debate and discouraging lengthy discussion. She knew how to unwind naturally, and

this spared her much useless fatigue. The aptness of her remarks and her behaviour astonished all those who knew her.[32]

Ruth Harris says Bernadette is important to Lourdes because she was herself:

> Despite the many constraints, despite the emotions and spiritual qualities that visitors projected on to her, her few written words and interactions showed that she would only go so far before she resisted. She did so quietly and persistently, revealing a quiet charisma, a sure gaze, a conviction of the truth of her story, a stalwart and dignified rejection of gifts and a simple generosity that stunned those who knew her poverty.[33]

During the apparitions and all the initial witnessing to what happened, we must remember that Bernadette was only fourteen years of age. Whenever she could, she loved to get away and play with her friends. She was a happy young girl with a practical sense of humour, which she retained. She could move from giving matter-of-fact answers to an 'important person', to running down the street laughing with her companions. She was real.

In July 1860, two years after the apparitions, Bernadette moved to the hospice. This was a positive move, providing her shelter from people's constant curiosity. It also gave her the chance to attend school regularly, though she was never very fond of the books. It was difficult for her leaving her family, as it was for them to see her go, but

---

32. Laurentin, *Bernadette of Lourdes*, 1979, p. 102.

33. Harris, *Lourdes: Body and Spirit in the Secular Age*, 2000, p. 140.

she did visit them regularly for the next six years while she was in Lourdes.

On 7 December 1860, Bernadette was summoned for a final interrogation before the bishop and his commission. She acquitted herself well as usual. The high point was when she was asked to show how exactly the Virgin spoke the words, 'I am the Immaculate Conception'. She stood up, stretched out her arms, joined her hands and said the words. This had a profound effect on the bishop and the others. On 18 January 1862, the bishop issued his official letter recognising the apparitions: 'We judge that the Immaculate Mother of God truly appeared to Bernadette.'[34] The judgement was grounded on the spiritual fruits of the events in Lourdes, on the cures and on Bernadette herself.

What is God Asking?

NOW HER ATTENTION TURNED MORE TO WHAT SHE should do for the rest of her life. She was confident early on that she wanted to be a religious Sister, but in what congregation was a different matter. Several congregations were interested in her, but she had a mind of her own and was not going to decide too quickly. She was worried about how her health could stop her doing what she wanted. Her lack of money was also a worry. Then she was not sure how she could be of use in any congregation. She found she was attracted to serving the sick and the poor in the hospice when she was able. All this time, Dean Peyramale, who had been one

---

34. Jean-Paul Lefebvre-Filleau, *L'Affaire Bernadette Soubirous*, Paris: Cerf, 1997, p. 155.

of her harshest critics, now was a great support to her. Eventually she decided to ask to be admitted into the Congregation of the Sisters of Charity of Nevers, who ran the hospice. One reason she gave for that choice was that they did not press her and she felt they respected her freedom.[35]

On 4 July 1866, Bernadette left Lourdes and arrived in Nevers on 7 July. She was now twenty-two years of age. She lived the remainder of her life – thirteen years – in that convent, the mother house of the congregation. She found there a chance to escape from a lot of curiosity, but not all. The Sisters protected her from the curious but not as much as Bernadette would have liked. She remained in poor health, and indeed received the last rites on at least three occasions during those years.

The spirituality of the time and the superiors were very concerned about the dangers of pride. Bernadette's superiors regarded her celebrity as a serious danger to her growth in holiness. When she received the religious habit three weeks after arriving in Nevers she was given the name of St Marie-Bernard. The rest of the novices were scattered all over France to complete their formation in the local houses of congregation. Bernadette was kept in Nevers to protect her from the curious. Then in October 1867, on the occasion of her religious profession, two authorities felt there was another side to the solution. 'The tasks in the mother-house were regarded as the "top jobs in the congregation." Only in an exceptional case would newly professed nuns be assigned there.'[36]

---

35. Actes du Colloque de 'l'Année Bernadette', Bruyères-le-Châtel: Nouvelle Cité, 2009, p. 21.

36. Laurentin, *Bernadette of Lourdes*, 1979, p. 160.

So in the presence of all, including her forty-three fellow novices, when the bishop came to announce the convent where Bernadette would serve, he said:

'Sister Marie-Bernarde – nowhere.'
Then he spoke directly to Bernadette.
'Is it true, Sister, that you are good for nothing?'
'Yes, it's true.'
'Well then my poor child, what are we going to do with you?'
'Well, I told you that in Lourdes when you wanted to get me to enter the community and you replied that it would not matter.' ...
The bishop assumed a graver tone and spoke out solemnly:
'I give you the job of prayer.'[37]

Bernadette's devotion to Mary and her sense of Mary's protection were constants in her life. As she was either helping in the infirmary, in charge of it, or a patient in it, she had a lot of contact with the community. She often attended the recreation of the novices and her superiors were very happy that she do so, feeling that the novices would benefit from contact with her. She was focused on loving God and on loving the other Sisters, especially on loving the sick patients in the infirmary. In her responsibilities in the infirmary she was very competent. It is important to remember that she was canonised not because she had visions at the age of fourteen, but because of the faith, hope and love she lived in the midst

---

37. Ibid., p. 160.

of poverty, service, adulation, suffering and the ordinary events of day-to-day life. She lived ordinary life with simplicity until her death at the age of thirty-five.

There is no doubt her friendship with the Immaculate Conception helped her see things from God's perspective, and that the joy and the beauty of the grotto enriched her understanding of God's grace and favour. She was also conscious of the sadness caused by sin and the failure of people to do God's will. When her suffering increased in the final years and final days, she found strength in looking on her crucified Lord. She just wanted to return his love and with him offer everything, first for her own sins and then for all sinners. She was so aware of the need of those who were caring for her. Bernadette would ask the sister who was attending her at night not to trouble herself and to get some sleep. Many of the sisters were grateful to her for her understanding and encouragement.

From 1875 her sickness became central to her life. She said that sickness was her work.[38] On 30 October 1878, the infirmary for professed nuns was opened on the first floor and soon after Bernadette took up permanent residence in her 'white chapel', as she called her big curtained bed. One picture near the bed symbolised the Masses being said around the clock all over the world. 'I unite myself with all these Masses, especially during the night when I sometimes get no sleep,' she told one sister.[39] When she remarked to a sister that she found the inactivity very hard, she was told: 'You pray for those

---

38. Ibid., p. 178.
39. Ibid., p. 189.

who do not pray.' 'That is all I have to do ... My prayer is my only weapon. I can only pray and suffer.'[40] She inspired them in so many ways and they cared for her with affection and love. Being born into a milling family, it is only apt that she should use the following metaphor to express her suffering: 'I am being ground like a grain of corn between two millstones.'

Bernadette was very anxious to care for others, especially the sick and those in need. She found it very hard to be the one who was being cared for, and felt bad about being a burden on others. Her concern for others and her appreciation of their kindness were remembered with deep gratitude by her community. She retained her sense of humour and her own self-confidence through all the difficulties. She enjoyed friendship. She had a special relationship with the Sisters from her own region and enjoyed receiving news from Lourdes. While she had confidence that she would be rewarded with happiness, she felt in her final years that her 'passion will last until the end'. Her hope was the victory of Christ on the cross and the intercession of Mary for sinners, herself first, and then others.

Bernadette died on Easter Wednesday, 1879. She was beatified in 1925 and canonised in 1933. At her baptism she was recognised as a member of the parish and a child of God. Now she was recognised as someone who allowed the Holy Spirit recreate her as a friend and model for us all, especially when we have the grace to recognise our weaknesses and failure to love as we might, and when we open our hearts to the joy and beauty God is offering.

---

40. Ibid., p. 190.

Centre of Prayer and Pilgrimage

THE PARISH OF LOURDES ON THE MORNING OF 11 February 1858 was already a field cultivated by the grace of God. Still, nobody planned the events that unfolded when the Soubirous family needed fuel for the fire. First, it was a new journey for Bernadette. Then the parish of Lourdes and neighbouring parishes got involved. We have sketched the story of how Bernadette's friendship with Mary led her to the heart of the life of the Father, Son and Holy Spirit, the fulfilment of her baptism. We have also sketched the determination of the local people to witness to their faith and the unexpected presence of grace among them. It was this local faith community who first came to the grotto to pray. They believed Mary, the Mother of God, was near. It was they who came singing litanies of Mary that they had learnt during May devotions. It was they who first drew water from the well in faith and hope of healing. It was they who first brought their sick to wash in the water. It was they who first worked on the site to make it more accessible and welcoming. These local people saw all this as part of their parish where they celebrated the sacraments and learned their faith.

The first official ceremony at the grotto at Lourdes took place on 4 April 1864, when the statue at the grotto was blessed. Fifteen thousand people, followed by Bishop Laurence and 120 priests, walked in procession from the parish church to the grotto. The preacher praised the faithful for having yielded to the attraction of God's grace among them. Already, with the support of the mayor of Lourdes, the bishop had bought a lot of the land immediately around the grotto. The way was now cleared to begin work on building the chapel asked for by the Lady.

The opening of the railway line from Bordeaux to Lourdes in June 1867 was a major event. The first special pilgrimage train arrived from Bayonne in July of that year with seven hundred pilgrims. Another milestone was a French national pilgrimage, from 5–8 October 1872, when 25,000 pilgrims arrived with banners flying representing every part of France. During that year the number of pilgrims to Lourdes reached 119,000.

In 1873, the records of the Railway Company show that 140,000 pilgrims visited Lourdes. These came not only from France, but from Spain and Belgium as well. The sick were not specifically catered for in these first pilgrimages but people became very aware of their presence. In 1874, fourteen sick people who could not afford to pay for the journey were brought on the national pilgrimage and the foundation stone of St Frai, the Hospital of Our Lady of Sorrows, was laid.

From the beginning, the sick brought by their families stayed in various lodging houses and were cared for by their families and friends. From 1862, a shelter was built to enable the sick to wash themselves at the fountain. By 1883, Lourdes was able to accommodate one thousand sick during the French National Pilgrimage. This growth was achieved due to a great commitment from religious and lay volunteers. From very early on, various congregations were involved in the life of the shrine. In France, the role of two congregations – the Congregation of the Assumption Fathers and the Little Sisters of the Assumption – was particularly important in building up the place of Lourdes in the life of the nation. To get a sense of the scale of the challenge in rather difficult conditions, it is enough to recall that in 1880 there were four thousand pilgrims on the French National Pilgrimage, including 917 sick who were not asked to pay. That year, the beginnings of the Hospitalité emerged in Lourdes and the Officiel Hospitalité de Notre-Dame de Lourdes was established in 1885. Today it is an association of Christian volunteers who welcome and accompany thousands of pilgrims each year at Lourdes.

From very early on, people from Ireland were finding their way to the grotto. In 1883 the Oblates of Mary Immaculate organised the first pilgrimage from Ireland. Then in 1913, the first National Pilgrimage from Ireland travelled to Lourdes. Another National Pilgrimage to Lourdes was led by Cardinal MacRory in 1933, the year of Bernadette's canonisation. The largest pilgrimage from Ireland now is the Annual Dublin Diocesan Pilgrimage, which has over two thousand participants each year. Most other dioceses have a diocesan pilgrimage, as have many religious orders and congregations. There is also a continuous stream of parish and local pilgrims from all over the country.

One obvious mark of Lourdes on the Irish landscape are the Lourdes grottos all over the country, many of which are cherished and colourful features of the area. Perhaps of greater significance in the popular mind is the association of Lourdes with prayer. The great salute of people to someone setting off on pilgrimage is so often: 'Pray for us in Lourdes!' and on arriving home: 'Did you pray for us?'

Part Two

REFLECTIONS

IN THE SECOND PART OF THIS BOOK I WILL REFLECT on how the life of Bernadette, and those who were part of her journey, opened up so many possibilities of faith, hope and love for millions of people. The role of the poorer people in the community was central. It is hard not to think of the words of St Paul: 'It was to shame the wise that God chose what is foolish by human reckoning, and to shame what is strong that he chose what is weak by human reckoning; ... those who are nothing at all to show up those who are everything' (1 Cor 1:27, 28).

In reflecting on the founding experiences of Lourdes as a centre of prayer and pilgrimage, our model is Mary who accepted her role as the Mother of God and valued all that happened to her. 'As for Mary, she treasured all these things and pondered them in her heart' (Lk 2:19). Bernadette too accepted her part in the Father's plan, and learned to know herself as a beloved child and sister to so many. Her life was a seed planted in God's field, and it is still bearing fruit.

Made in God's Image

WHEN I AM TAKING PEOPLE ON A WALKING TOUR IN Lourdes and it comes to the part of the story where her older female cousin was making no headway in her efforts to get thirteen-year-old Bernadette to learn her French Catechism answers off by heart, I remark that Bernadette must be the patron saint of all who were told they are stupid by those who set out to teach them. There is a bigger issue raised by the wisdom and realism of Bernadette: at a very young age she had such a grasp of her dignity and such conviction that as long as she was telling the truth she had no reason to fear that we might ask where did all this come from?

So often in Lourdes when people are reflecting on the meaning of what is going on, they remember the words of Jesus: 'Come to me, all you who labour and are overburdened, and I will give you rest. Shoulder my yoke and learn from me, for I am gentle and humble in heart and you will find rest for your souls' (Mt 11:28, 29). It is good when we pay attention to these words of the Lord. However, just before he issues that invitation, we see Jesus in a great state of excitement as he exclaims: 'I bless you, Father, Lord of heaven and of earth, for hiding these things from the learned and the clever and revealing them to mere children. Yes, Father, for that is what it pleased you to do' (Mt 11:25). The situation gets more challenging when Jesus says: 'Let the little children come to me, and do not stop them; for it is to such as these that the Kingdom of God belongs. I tell you solemnly, anyone who does not welcome the Kingdom of God like a little child will never enter it' (Mt 19:14).

George Bernanos, the great French writer, has a really challenging comment on this. Writing in the autograph album of a young girl, he said:

Remain faithful to the poets, remain faithful to childhood! Never become an important person! There is a conspiracy among important people against childhood, and it is enough to read the Gospels to recognise this. The good God said to cardinals, theologians, essayists, historians, novelists, indeed to everybody: 'Become like children.' And the cardinals, theologians, essayists, novelists, repeat century after century to betrayed childhood: 'Become like us.' When you read these lines, many years from now, remember and say a prayer for the old writer who believes more and more in the powerlessness of the powerful, the ignorance of the Doctors, the silliness of the Machiavellians, and the incurable frivolity of serious people. All that which is beautiful in the history of the world is done unknown to us by the mysterious accord between the humble and ardent patience of people and the gentle mercy of God.[41]

One of the common remarks about Bernadette that fascinates me is the idea that she was an enigma. At the age of fourteen she had so little schooling that she was constantly referred to as ignorant. Her health was so poor that she was given to understand that she was useless. Because she could not learn slabs of French off by heart for her First Communion she was told she was stupid.

41. Albert Béguin, *Bernanos par lui-même*, Paris: Éditions du Seuil, 1958, p. 96.

She was looked down on for the poverty of her family and for their being 'known to the police'. These social assumptions and the way they undermined people's respect for her were heavy burdens. Still she had her own dignity as a human being.

If people had more respect for humanity, things might have been easier for Bernadette. Today, it is hard for young people who are made to feel that dignity is dependent on success or possessions. It is hard on all of us. Bernadette cannot be understood in terms of labels; neither can any of the rest of us.

The abiding memory of almost all who examine the evidence as regards Bernadette as a witness was that she was so real. She was happy to be herself, secure and sincere, with common sense, charm and a very natural humour.

I love the joy of liberation on people's faces when they stand in the Cachot as pilgrims and wonder at all that Bernadette did with her life without material wealth. Young people seem to think about it all in a quieter, more contemplative way. One of the great prophets of the twentieth century was a Belgian priest called Joseph Cardijn. He founded the worldwide movement of the Young Christian Workers. Thousands of young workers' lives were totally transformed by this movement. He founded everything on what he called the truth of faith: 'Every young worker has a unique call in life, a unique meaning in his or her life.' In the context of the story of Bernadette, it is interesting that his first collaborators in the founding of this movement in 1910 were young girls working in terrible conditions in factories. He could see that each one of them had a dignity totally independent of their health, their lack of education, success or possessions. Blessed John Paul said that: 'In reality, the name for that deep amazement at man's worth and dignity is the Gospel, that is to say: the Good News. It is also called Christianity.'[42] Bernadette was blessed with the way Christianity was lived in her family and her parish. She was blessed in her confidence in prayer. She was surely blessed in her ability to rejoice in the beauty of friendship and in her ability to be glad of the respect and courtesy shown to her, and draw life from it all. She was in touch with nourishment that enabled her to withstand being underestimated by 'the learned and the clever'. She would have been at ease with the poet who sang:

How great the tale that there should be
In God's Son's heart a place for me,
That on a sinner's lips like mine
The cross of Jesus Christ should shine.[43]

When I watch the stream of people passing through the grotto in solemn silence, I wonder at the millions of people, each with his or her own life story, who have made their way to Lourdes since that first February morning in 1858. From the beginning they came because of an internal impulse. They know that here you will not be asked about your examination results or your bank balance or how many friends you have on social media sites. It is really a wondrous procession of humanity. More than four million come each year now. This grotto and its story says to all: 'You too are invited, and even if

42. John Paul II, *Redemptor Hominis*, 26.
43. Quoted in the Breviary, Vol. 1, p. 140.

for whatever reason you and God are not on great terms at the moment, come anyway. And you can drink freely from the water and take some with you as well.' As the great Jewish prophet said long ago: 'Oh, come to the water all you who are thirsty; though you who have no money, come' (Is 55:1).

There is nobody like you. They might be similar to you but they are not you. You have something nobody else has got. You are something else! And as it says in Jeremiah: 'Before I formed you in the womb, I knew you, before you came to birth I consecrated you' (1:5).

The short and the long of it is that in your life something new is happening. We have all received our human heritage in a unique way. Then we have our experiences. Some of these we feel good about at the time, but later feel differently. Others are painful at the time but we might be so glad about them later. Each of these experiences can add to our potential to grow in humanity.

To know something as a fact is one thing, but to know it deep down and grasp it with personal conviction in a way that enables us to grow is quite another. We owe so much to those who help us realise how special and unique we are! We owe a great debt to those who cherish us with their eyes and we know it is the language of the heart that we are reading in their eyes. Of course, we can be blind at times. We can be deaf. We can be in situations where love and affection surround us, yet we are not receiving. We can be locked into other wavelengths that are not nurturing us but seem very attractive and likeable.

For many reasons, countless people feel unsure of themselves today. Their sense of self-worth can be undermined by many of the assumptions regarding education, health, social status, success and so on. Bernadette drew from deeper wells. She was the victim of so many assumptions about what makes the dignity of a human being. She knew what a fragile economic situation can do to a family. We can look to her to give us a healthier perspective on the dignity of all.

Free to Belong

FROM THE BEGINNING, THE GROTTO IN LOURDES attracted people. They were drawn out of curiosity and many found themselves praying both with their neighbours and with strangers. It was a gathering that nobody planned or controlled, though many individuals had an influence on the growth of the phenomenon. It fascinates me that the people gathered in reverential prayer at the site, and as soon as the apparition was over, they stood up and spoke eagerly to each other. Those who had been strangers were now at ease with one another; they were an extended family. That gathering of individuals into community has continued to be central to the life of the shrine of Lourdes. There is so much practical, mutual help among the pilgrims themselves; so many talents being put to use for the generous service of others; so much sharing of stories and life's hopes and fears; so many having time to listen and share; and again the scriptures are being fulfilled as people continue to bear one another's burdens (cf. Gal 6:2). When the young people make friends with the sick on the diocesan pilgrimage they are part of a living stream of human flourishing that has been flowing since Bernadette first went to gather sticks where the pigs used to shelter. A space is continually created where people can refresh their outlook on life.

When on a Lourdes pilgrimage, there is much remembrance and prayer for people at home – for all their needs and hopes. Many of those who have died are also remembered in a living communion of saints. These trips can take a lot of organising and hours of planning and hard work. Many prayers are offered for those at home who make it all possible. Their generosity is truly appreciated. And it is not a question of Lourdes being the embodiment of the pure communion of people in comparison to home and all the struggles and problems associated with day-to-day living. Still, a lot of the celebratory comments people pass in Lourdes regard the time people have for others that they might find difficult to find at home. These days we are becoming more and more aware of how fragile we human beings can be, how many can feel depressed or dangerously isolated at times. People who feel the burden of this stress find Lourdes a breath of fresh air.

When we pray the Our Father, we say, 'Your will be done on earth' (Mt 6:9). It is great when we have even the slightest awareness that we are the children of God. It is great when we make even the slightest effort to live together as God wills. From the beginning, Jesus Christ wanted to unite those who were learning to trust his invitation to a new life, he wanted them to be one. He told them: 'By this love you have for one another everyone will know that you are my disciples' (Jn 13:35). He really wanted them to live a togetherness that was drawing its inspiration and energy from the life he lived 'at home' with the Father in the Holy Spirit. 'As the Father has loved me, so I have loved you' (Jn 15:9).

One of the great words the early Christians had for this togetherness was the Greek word *koinonia*, which is translated in English as 'communion' or 'fellowship'. *Koinonia* was the word for the unity of the Lord Jesus Christ with his heavenly Father. It was also the word for the unity lived among those learning the way of Jesus. 'The whole group of believers was united heart and soul. No one claimed for his own use anything that he had, as everything they owned was held in common' (Acts 4:32).

In the first letter of John, this is put very simply: 'What we have seen and heard we are telling you, so that you too may be in union with us as we have union with the Father and with his Son Jesus Christ. We are writing this to you to make our own joy complete' (1 Jn 1:3-4). When we remember what the angels said to the shepherds on the first Christmas night we see that the word of God is an invitation to respond to good news and to welcome joy. That night the angels announced: 'I bring you news of great joy, joy to be shared by the whole people' (Lk 2:10).

From the beginning, people have used words like 'heavenly' when they try to describe their experience of Lourdes. They often refuse to put words on their experience because they say it is 'something out of this world'. I think the healing power of the joyous experience of Lourdes is a real contact with the deeper life of God's people.

The first Christians recognised themselves as those gathered by God's word, or as those called by God. This is where the Greek word *ekklesia* (the called), or the Irish word *eaglais*, meaning church, come from. Down through the centuries, those called by God, through the Church, have had many high points and low points. Still, in all their fragility, there were some who remembered the belonging they were called to. At the centre of this sense of being called by God was the celebration of what the Lord did on the night he was betrayed. At this gathering to recall the words, death and resurrection of the Lord, the community was renewed in its identity and hope. At this gathering they recalled the words of the Risen Christ who was crucified for all, that they may be witnesses to all – to what they had seen and heard – baptising them in the name of the Father, the Son and the Holy Spirit.

In Baptism we are plunged into a new life, the abundant life of the Trinity. We are asked to abandon the old patterns of sin and selfishness for a freedom to receive and to share. We are given the Holy Spirit to help us move out of self-centredness into fellowship and sharing. We are called to die and to rise anew, through the grace of Christ's self-giving that sins might be forgiven. When we are clothed in Christ at our baptism we receive the gift of a new identity, children of God, called to become more and more the son or daughter of God, and to live as brothers and sisters of each other. This is a lifelong challenge.

It might be easier to live as a Christian family during a pilgrimage to Lourdes, but even the ease and the joy of the companionship speaks to us of our deepest identity, what God is calling us to, where we see what it is all about.

Mary, the Mother of our Saviour, models for us the call of God, to belong in the family life of the Trinity. Bernanos said of Mary, the mother of Jesus, that she 'is younger than sin'.[44] The doctrine of the Immaculate Conception tells us that because of the sacrifice of her Son she was preserved from all trace of sin from the very moment of her conception. From the beginning she was clothed in the life of Christ. So it was fitting that she appeared to Bernadette as the beautiful young girl dressed in white. She is the one who models the fullness of our baptismal glory for us. She already enjoys what St Paul describes as God's choice of all of us: 'Before the world was made, he chose us, chose us in Christ, to be holy and spotless and to live through love in his presence' (Eph 1:4).

At our baptism each one of us received a white robe and the priest prayed:

> You have become a new creature, clothed in Christ. See in this white garment the outward sign of your Christian dignity. With your family and friends to you by word and example, may you gain everlasting life.

The friend of Bernadette, in the form of a beautiful young girl dressed in white, is our friend too, and where she has gone we are called by our Heavenly Father, 'to make us praise the glory of his grace' (Eph 1:6). One grace that is on offer in Lourdes is a glimpse of the glory of our baptismal call and a glimpse of what we are all called to live together in our own parishes at home.

This is an offer from God. However, it is a gift that needs our openness to love. Could I try for a moment to

44. Béguin, *Bernanos par lui-même*, 1958, p. 42.

look at things from God's point of view: from the point of view of a father who will never forget me. He gave me a unique life to live, and he is very fond of me and would love to see me respond to the best promptings of my own heart more often. I remember one day a parishioner arrived at my house with his eight-year-old son to pick up some chairs and transport them by car trailer down the street to the local hall. When they were ready to move, the young boy wanted to mount the heap of chairs on the trailer and ride in triumph through the village. His father naturally felt it safer for his son to ride in the car. I felt I should show solidarity with the father, so I said to the boy: 'It is because your Dad is fond of you that he wants you to travel down to the hall in the car.' To which I got the very emotional reply: 'I don't like people who are fond of me – they never let me do anything fun!'

Personal freedom is not simple. It is a gift from God. I can use it to ignore God. I can use it in ways that diminish myself. We are so quick to feel our freedom is threatened, especially from those who seem to be too fond of us. I often think of that sensitive line from Jesus to Peter: 'Do you want to go away too?' (Jn 6:67). Jesus has poured out his heart telling people that he would give his life as food for people to eat and his life as drink for their thirst. The crowds don't accept it and walk away. Jesus turns to Peter with his question, and I am amazed when I try to imagine the feelings and the face of Jesus. He has come to bring good news. He is losing the crowds. He is now waiting for Peter's decision. At the heart of his situation, however, is the challenge to respect the dignity of his Father's creation. He must show total respect for Peter's freedom. There must be no manipulation, no flattery –

just a question from one friend to another. It is the same for us. Like Peter, Jesus asks us – will you too go away? It is our decision, our free choice, how we respond.

Penance

IT ALWAYS MEANT SO MUCH TO BERNADETTE THAT her first and abiding sense of her experience with the vision was reverence, respect, friendship, joy and beauty. Although those who were first drawn to the grotto by Bernadette did not see any vision, it was a similar sense of wonder that inspired them. Today, thousands are still experiencing a similar peace and grace.

In contrast to these fundamental aspects of the life of the grotto in Lourdes, another dimension was introduced at the eighth apparition on 24 February, when the vision used a new word, 'Penance' and asked Bernadette to 'Pray to God for the conversion of sinners'.[45] As she spoke about these matters, the vision, who was normally so joyful, was now rather sad.[46] The significant interruption of the peace and joy of the grotto was caused by the recognition of the reality of sin and sinners. When we fail in our response to God's call to love we are on the side of sadness. We are not born for sadness. God sent his Son among us saying that he came that his 'joy would be in you and that your joy be complete' (Jn 15:11).

The great prophet of penance was John the Baptist, who came to prepare a way for the Lord. For a long time I had a rather negative opinion of John the Baptist. I considered him a rather grumpy character who was out

45. Laurentin, *Bernadette of Lourdes*, 1979, p. 58.

46. Laurentin, *Histoire Authentique des Apparitions*, Vol. 3, 1961, p. 179.

to make us feel small. I suppose I brought some of this with me in my reaction to the call to penance in Lourdes. It was a breakthrough for me when I discovered that John the Baptist is calling us to new possibilities. He is a person of conviction with a great sense of the dignity and nobility of each person in God's eyes.

Today Lourdes invites each one of us to reconsider the image we have of ourselves and our potential. We all need to wonder about ourselves from time to time!

There is a story about a man from a big city who bought a field at the side of a mountain. He looked out his window one morning and saw a local man walking across the field. He decided to act on this trespassing immediately and challenged the trespasser: 'What are you doing here?' The man paused, looked at him gently and replied calmly: 'That is a very good question! What are any of us doing here?'

If you are ever in Lourdes and you are having a quiet moment, you too might ask: 'What am I doing in this world?' For a start you might recognise yourself as a field, which has had a lot of cultivation already; cultivation in which the Holy Spirit has had a bigger part than you might imagine. Perhaps, with a different type of cultivation, you might have the potential to produce new fruits.

The word 'penance' is key in the story of Lourdes. I suppose we tend to see the need to change and the value of change as being something for 'serious sinners'. But, for a moment, could we stay with that image of one's life as a field: perhaps a field that more or less meets my own expectations and those of others around me, but that would respond surprisingly well to new cultivation.

In St John's Gospel there is the account of Jesus meeting a woman at the well and having the longest recorded conversation he had with anyone. Jesus asks her for a drink. The woman is surprised by the openness of Jesus to her as a person. She is taken aback when she realises that Jesus knows she has had five husbands and that she is not married to her present partner. Jesus says to her something he says to each one of us when we are slow to respond: 'If you only knew what God is offering!' (Jn 4:10). In this meeting, someone who had been wounded is touched and she risks changing her outlook. Now she recognises herself as a person asked to call people to the Messiah, and she receives a new respect from the people in her town.

Recently, I was very touched by a report from somebody who has listened to a lot of people who have been abused. He said that in some cases he found that a person was most grateful, even more than when they got practical help or good advice, when they could say: 'Today, I met a human being who listened to me!' The human need to have one's words respected is a very deep part of what we are. We are reminded of how utterly human Jesus became when he said to us: 'If anyone loves me he will keep my words and my Father will love him and we shall come to him and make our home with him' (Jn 14:23). Jesus always treasured his bond with his heavenly Father as the source and goal of his life. When we listen to and put his words into practice he promises to share what is most precious in his life.

I sometimes feel that those who say they want to help people in need because it is a Christian act, but who have no interest in going to church, might be surprised to learn how much Jesus longs to be listened to by them. Jesus is a lover who wants to be heard by the ones he loves. He is the one often ignored who wants to be heard by a human heart.

There is something amiss when a person feels that they are on their own. There is so much love longing for a human ear and a human heart. Saint Augustine spoke for many when he said: 'You have made us for yourself, O Lord, and our hearts are restless until they rest in you.' We are now learning that there is a corresponding restlessness in the heart of God to rest in you and me. When we see Christianity as a list of obligations and prohibitions, we can often wonder: is that all? When we treasure the words of Jesus and turn them over in our hearts, we can glimpse a new perspective. The perspective of Jesus is one of thanksgiving and self-giving, of forgiveness and community, of belonging and sharing.

I remember once talking and listening to a small group of young adults who were reviewing their weekends. One mentioned the great welcome he met at the door when he returned home on Friday evening. One of the listeners wanted to know who this welcoming person was, and of this person, she exclaimed: 'She is a fountain of love!' Then someone asked, 'Are we not all called to be fountains of love?' This drew the very rapid comment: 'Yes, but sometimes the plumbing gets blocked!'

Though an outside plumber is not able to do much here, the tender joy of God stands at the door knocking. We received the freedom from somewhere to lock ourselves in and lock the plumber out! Still the Holy Spirit is always around to remind us of what Jesus said: 'Look, I am standing at the door, knocking. If one of you hears me calling and opens the door, I will come in to share his meal, side by side with him' (Rv 3:20).

In his pastoral letter to the Catholics of Ireland, Pope Benedict XVI spoke of Friday Penance and of fasting, prayer, reading of Sacred Scripture and works of mercy as prayer for an outpouring of God's mercy. He wanted to encourage people to discover anew the Sacrament of Reconciliation and to avail themselves more frequently of the transforming power of its grace.

There is also a moment of grace in that sense of gratitude that many people have when on Friday we often hear: 'Thank God it's Friday.' If enough Christians could imagine Friday as the day of thanksgiving for having employment and rest in their lives, it might be a reason to see Friday as the day of preparation for our Saturday evening or Sunday morning Mass. Sunday is the Lord's Day, the day we are invited to remember all we have received, and we are plunged again into our baptismal identity as children of our heavenly Father and sisters and brothers of each other. It is the great well of life for our faith, hope and love.

To prepare for Easter, the Church asks us to take a responsible part in the joyful season of Lent as we are asked to shake off all that has distracted us from living our faith in the past year and come to remember again the glory of who we are in God's heart. In a similar way, we are encouraged to free up the hope and joy of our souls for the Lord's Day by what we do on Friday.

Friday is the memory of the Lord's pouring out his life for us. As our bishops reminded us in their pastoral regarding penance: 'The link between Friday and penance is extremely ancient and is even reflected in the Irish word for Friday, *An Aoine* (the fast).' It is a fasting from some things to allow space for new choices. It might help if we see penance as a turning from negativity to opening up space for positivity.

The founding events of Lourdes took place around Lent and Easter 1858. During that time many people in the parish of Lourdes got more involved in consciously living their faith. Penance is a way of choosing and expressing our choice in action. As the story of Lourdes illustrates, it is a personal matter with consequences for many, many others. For Bernadette, it was about opening a way for joy where there was already too much sadness.

There are many items on the traditional Lenten menu from which to choose what give us life: abstaining from meat or some other food; abstaining from alcoholic drink or smoking; making a special effort at involvement in family prayer; making a special effort to participate in Mass on Fridays; visiting the Blessed Sacrament; making the Stations of the Cross; fasting from all food for a longer period than usual and perhaps giving what is saved to the needy; helping the poor, sick, old or lonely.[47]

Friday was the day Our Saviour chose to put us first. Maybe we could make it a day when we try to put him first by reading and reflecting on the word of God. There are many groups and resources available to help you explore the world of the Bible. It is a great and challenging pilgrimage on which you will learn a lot about yourself and God and meet many wonderful

---

47. Irish Catholic Bishops' Conference, Friday Penance pastoral, 2012.

people. We can always start by listening to and thinking about the Sunday readings. Most parishes are delighted if you take the Mass leaflet home with you for the week.

'Thank God it's Friday' could be a diving deeper into the mystery and wonder of our lives, as we try, to paraphrase Patrick Kavanagh, to 'charm back the luxury ... that was in every stale thing'.[48]

Christ, 'holy, innocent, and undefiled' (Heb 7:26) knew nothing of sin, but came only to expiate the sins of the people. The Church ... at once holy and always in need of purification, follows constantly the path of penance and renewal. All members of the Church, including her ministers, must acknowledge that they are sinners ... the Church gathers sinners already caught up in Christ's salvation but still on the way to holiness.[49]

Being Aware

DURING THE APPARITIONS, BERNADETTE DID NOT make it easy for people by insisting that she did not know who the vision was. Many were saying from the beginning that it was the Blessed Virgin. Of course they had the idea that the Blessed Virgin was a very stately lady. Bernadette's insistence that she was seeing a young girl who smiled a lot and spoke to her as one person

---

48. The full verse from Kavanagh reads: 'But here in this Advent-darkened room/Where the dry black bread and the sugarless tea/Of penance will charm back the luxury/Of a child's soul ... And the newness that was in every stale thing/When we looked at it as children: ...' From 'Advent', *Patrick Kavanagh: Collected Poems*, Antoinette Quinn, ed., London: Allen Lane, 2004, pp. 110–111.

49. *Catechism of the Catholic Church*, 827.

speaks with another was a challenge to their image of Our Lady. The people could see that Bernadette loved being treated with courtesy. During the apparitions her appearance was transformed and her coughing stopped. All this quiet affirmation and positive experience must have been part of what gave her such self-assurance and the freedom to be so real with herself and others.

When we are trying to lead each other in learning to grasp the faith, or even helping each other to allow the faith to grasp us, we might consider the elements of the relationship between Bernadette and the beautiful girl. There was an atmosphere of prayer that was introduced by a very solemn making of the sign of the cross. Onlookers noted that this was followed by greetings and salutations that were a very important part of the developing relationship. In the rosary there was a reflection on the lived mysteries of Christ's life. There was friendly conversation warmed with smiles and signs of respect. There was the confidence placed in Bernadette that she could receive a message and pass it on. She was being trusted with responsibility in the community. The apparitions were a community experience. From early on, Bernadette was accompanied by the prayers of her neighbours. This experience of solidarity and hospitable friendship must have been important to Bernadette. It challenges us all to think about the place of hospitality and friendship in faith formation and in parish life.

Perhaps also in our own growth in faith, we need to look at the space in our own lives for reaching out to others in hospitality and friendship. That might help us understand why it was so important to Bernadette.

Sometimes we might feel that learning God's will is something completely separate from what is happening in our lives and in the lives of those around us. Mary, Bernadette and the founding of Lourdes as a great centre of prayer and pilgrimage tell a different story. Those Christians in the parish of Lourdes and the diocese of Tarbes had to struggle with actual events and the accounts people were giving of those events. In this they were following the example of Mary, as she is presented to us by St Luke, who tells us twice that she was a deep thinker. At the end of the account of all the events that led up to the birth of Jesus, right up to and including the visit of the shepherds, St Luke says: 'As for Mary she treasured all these things, and pondered them in her heart' (Lk 2:19). Again, at the end of the story of Jesus' childhood, including the finding in the temple, St Luke says: 'His mother stored up all these things in her heart' (Lk 2:51). Her treasuring of her personal experiences and her pondering them in her heart is an invitation and challenge to all of us to respect the mystery of our own daily experiences, to reflect on them and to see them as part of our way to God.

People of faith are often accused of not taking the realities of this world seriously enough. Mary, Bernadette and the people of Lourdes respected their experiences and pondered them in their hearts to find there the generous saving will of our God. They all challenge us to take our experience in Lourdes seriously, and amidst different voices, different meetings and conversations, to listen with our hearts for the word of God.

Mary and Bernadette lived their spirituality in the midst of ordinary events. They were aware of what was happening and they shared in friendship. Bernadette felt she had to insist that Mary spoke with her 'like we are talking to each other now'. Bernadette lived her spirituality with open eyes. She would have agreed with the sentiments, even if she would never have used the words, of the founder of the Little Sisters of Jesus. Little Sister Magdeleine told her Fraternities: 'You will never be asked to keep your eyes lowered in the name of religious reserve, but instead to keep them wide open so as to see very clearly the suffering and misery of the world, as well as the beauty of life and of the entire universe.'[50]

In Lourdes today there are great mosaic images of the five Mysteries of Light that Blessed John Paul added to the rosary: The Baptism of Jesus, The Wedding of Cana, The Proclamation of the Kingdom of God, The Transfiguration and The Institution of the Eucharist. When you stand near the steps in the esplanade, or Rosary Square as it is also known, and look towards the Rosary Basilica, you can see these magnificent mosaics. The only one that has a representation of Mary is the Wedding of Cana. From the doors of the Basilica, the Lord and his mother greet us. It is not very hard to see what this has to say to us. First, there must be the words of Mary to the stewards: 'Do whatever he tells you' (Jn 2:5). Saint John tells us that this turning the water into wine at the wedding banquet was 'the first of the signs given by Jesus' (Jn 2:11). There are all kinds of hints about Jesus' ability to transform our lives too, hints that what Jesus is about is meeting us when we are down because of disappointment and embarrassment at our own failed calculations and offering us peace and the support of others.

---

50. *Following Brother Charles of Jesus, 'The Little Universal Brother'*, The Fraternity of the Little Sisters of Jesus, Rome, 1945, p. 22.

So much of what people find in Lourdes, with the help of Jesus and Mary, is foreshadowed in the wedding feast of Cana. They find a joy in togetherness, in fellowship, and a sign of God's plan to gather all his scattered children into his grace. The role of Mary was extraordinarily important in the life of Jesus. It is just as important in the life of the followers of Jesus who received her as mother at the foot of the cross. The role of any mother is a family role. When we look on her in the mosaic of the doors of the Rosary Basilica, as she sits at table with Jesus, we are looking at a shared love that has a place for each one of us. Mary and her Son invite all who enter the house of our heavenly Father to seek the love and joy that they know God is offering.

The Sick and the Needy

WHEN WE BEAR IN MIND THE POOR HEALTH OF Bernadette and how on that first morning on 11 February she was alone because her sickness prevented her from keeping up with the others, we see that the sick were always at the heart of Lourdes. Over the years the longings of the sick have been a constant presence in Lourdes. All come in hope of consolation, spiritual strength and peace. Many go away with a new sense of life. Since 1858, over seven thousand cures have been registered with the medical authorities in Lourdes. By 2008, sixty-seven of these have been recognised as miraculous by the Church. When one thinks of the human drama and new hope that is involved in these figures, it truly is remarkable.

For most of the sick, their visit to Lourdes is less dramatic. Still, many are glad they came. Lourdes is often a sign that they are important to their own local church community who organise things and generously defray their expenses. Being on pilgrimage can take a person out of their isolation. Other people, not just the helpers, have time for them. They are generally in the front rows at the ceremonies. In the care and attention they receive and in the companionship of the other sick they are helped in their faith. Many a person went to Lourdes and through seeing how others bear their burdens, their own attitudes change. In the sacrament of the sick they are reminded that Christ is their companion. They are invited to share with Christ in his self-offering for the human race.

Part of the burden of her ill health was Bernadette's sense of being a burden on others. She really would have preferred to be serving others than to be receiving their care. When I think of that, I wish I could help the sick imagine something of their enormous contribution to the life of this shrine of faith and pilgrimage, their contribution to the faith, hope and love of millions. Year after year, I hear young people talking about the encouragement they received from their contact with the sick. When people go on pilgrimage they are taking some time apart from their ordinary, daily concerns. When people set out for Lourdes they do so in the hope of some spiritual renewal. The presence of the sick opens up deeper questions for everybody; maybe some give more service but others share their courage and their faith. The pilgrimage becomes a journeying together as human beings. Year after year, I hear the hard-working organisers of the Lourdes pilgrimage say that it is the sick who make the pilgrimage. The reality of suffering is often beyond our understanding and easy explanations. Bernadette was sick for most of her short life and suffered terribly during her final years. She was not cured in Lourdes. As she was dying she clutched her crucifix. The cross of Christ was her hope.

When Blessed John Paul visited Lourdes in 1983, he recalled a famous story from the life of a cardinal archbishop of Paris, a story I first heard when I was a student. The cardinal was dying of cancer and he wrote to his priests saying: 'I have often written and spoken beautiful things about suffering. Now I cry.' Blessed John Paul continued: 'Just or unjust, wherever suffering is present, in spite of the partial explanations, it is difficult to understand and difficult to accept even for those who have faith.' Then he turns to the faith of the Church expressed by the Vatican Council: 'Through Christ and in Christ, the riddles of sorrow and death grow meaningful. Apart from his Gospel they overwhelm us.'[51]

Then Blessed John Paul offers three points of reflection to focus our thoughts:

First of all, whatever your suffering might be, whether it is physical or mental, personal or with the family, apostolic, even connected to the Church, what matters is that you see it clearly without minimising it, but, also, without letting it control you through the throwbacks it can create such as the feeling of failure, the futility of your life, etc. …

---

51. *Gaudium et Spes*, 22.

In his own life, Blessed John Paul also learned to know suffering and what a struggle it is for the human spirit. I find the second point he makes really challenging but surely very life-giving. He asks every person who is hurt by life to 'do something' if at all possible.

> If the Lord wishes to bring good from evil, it is because he invites you to be yourselves as active as you can, in spite of sickness and, if you are disabled, to take charge of yourself with the strength and the talents that you have, in spite of your disability. Those who surround you with their affection and mutual support like brotherhoods of the sick, seek sincerely that you love life and that it opens up in you again the sense of life as a gift of God.

We are all inspired when others 'take charge of themselves with the strength and talents that they have, in spite of disability'. They call us to do the same.

> Finally, the best part has yet to take place, the oblation. The offering won by the love of the Lord and our friends can allow us to achieve an even higher degree of theological charity, that is to lose oneself in the love of Christ and the Most Holy Trinity for humanity.[52]

These three stages, experienced by those who suffer according to their situation in life and the graces they have received, bring a wonderful interior freedom. This is the paradoxical teaching of the Gospel – 'anyone who

---

52. Address by John Paul II to the Sick, Lourdes, 15 August 1983, 3.

loses his life for my sake will find it' (Mt 16:25). Isn't this the dying to oneself of the Gospel, so deeply spoken of by Bernadette of Lourdes and Thérèse of Lisieux, who were sick almost all their lives? When we visit the struggles of the sick we are asked to be very humble, as we tread on holy ground.

Blessed John Paul then described the sick as very precious collaborators with Christ. This is such a reality in the everyday life of the shrine. In Lourdes, the sick play a central role in the work of strengthening people's faith. He told them that Mary, the Mother of Christ, will always be close to them.

As the sick and those who cared for them were drawn to the grotto from the very beginning, they were part of the great reality of Lourdes. Very early on it was found necessary to organise those who cared for the sick along certain structures. In the beginning the sick were cared for by their own families. As people were brought longer distances they stayed in local accommodation such as hotels and guesthouses, but they were still cared for by their own family members and friends. From the beginning of the 1870s with the arrival of large pilgrimage by train, this began to change.[53] The needs of the sick and especially the needs of people with little means led to special accommodation being built and the growth of groups committed to the care of the sick. A central expression of this development is the Hospitality of Our Lady of Lourdes. As well as serving the sick, the Hospitality is charged with helping its members grow in the Christian faith and

53. René Point, *Servir les Malades à Lourdes 1885–1985, 100 ans d'Hospitalité*, Lourdes: NDL Éditions, 2009, p. 12.

life. There is a great emphasis on the importance of a service that puts the needs of the sick first, in a way that inspires their confidence and trust through faithfulness and dependability. Members are asked to be willing to cooperate with the effort that is required in the situation. This calls for generosity of spirit and plenty of humility. While this service is terribly valuable it also carries an enormous responsibility to be faithful to the spirit with which Bernadette worked with the sick, and the call to recognise them as the sisters and brothers of the Lord, and indeed our own sisters and brothers in the family of Father, Son and Holy Spirit.

Bernadette's patient acceptance of her own suffering with asthma, especially at night, amazed her fellow Sisters. Their only memory of Bernadette complaining was about being cared for like a princess, with the often repeated comment: 'That is not how the poor are treated.'[54] She is inviting us all to consider how the poor are treated as a significant standard for our expectations and a monitor for our behaviour. Perhaps that could be a liberating consideration and an ennobling monitor.

We must not forget that Bernadette was at the grotto on that first day because of her poverty. Her early companions and the first to pray at the shrine were the poor. From the very beginning the poor were the receivers of the grace and light of Lourdes for all of us. While we can see the annunciation by the Angel Gabriel to Mary as a backdrop to Mary's appearing to Bernadette, we can also see the role of the poor in the Christmas story as a backdrop to the Lourdes story. The proclamation of

---

54. Laurentin, *Bernadette Vous Parle*, Tome 2, 1972, p. 304.

the Kingdom declares: 'Blessed are the poor in spirit for theirs is the Kingdom of God' (Mt 5:3). Our Saviour was rich but made himself poor for our sake.

After the Second World War, a lot of people turned to Lourdes for healing and new courage. In September 1946, Fr Jean Rodhain, the general chaplain to the thousands of French people who had been deported to Germany during the war, organised a great gathering in Lourdes for all these former prisoners. The effects of this pilgrimage had a lasting impact on Fr Rodhain. He went on to become the founding president of the Secours Catholique, the great movement in the French Church for the relief of those in need. In 1955, Monsignor Théas, Bishop of Tarbes and Lourdes, asked Fr Rodhain to set up an assistance centre for those who could not afford to pay to stay in a hotel while visiting Lourdes.[55] Now, 22,000 pilgrims are accommodated each year in the centre known as Cité St Pierre, or City of the Poor. Secours Catholique and Cité St Pierre challenge themselves to seek out the most vulnerable. Their presence is a reminder that the poor are central to the life of Lourdes.

Another revelation of how those in need continue to add to the wonder of Lourdes is the great gathering during Easter week of young people with special needs and their friends. During this week the Irish Pilgrimage Trust joins with their friends in the wider community of what started as the Handicapped Children's Pilgrimage Trust. Around five thousand pilgrims pray and celebrate, serve each other and socialise, with love, joy and wonder. The words of

---

55. *The Wonders of Lourdes: 150 Miraculous Stories of the Power of Prayer to Celebrate the 150th Anniversary of Our Lady's Apparition*, Gerald Korson, ed., John Pepino, trans., New York: Magnificat, 2008, p. 325.

Christ, 'I tell you solemnly, anyone who does not welcome the Kingdom of God like a little child will never enter it' (Lk 18:17), become a very life-giving challenge.

The historian Ruth Harris, summing up the story of Lourdes through all the turbulent years in France and western Europe over 150 years, sees the piety of the poor and the yearnings of the sick as the great source of sustenance for the life of the shrine.[56] It is important to remember in our pastoral planning that the Holy Spirit can have a different opinion to us as regards who it is best to look to for help and cooperation. Just because Bernadette was in poor health and in great need, this did not stop her being chosen for the great role she has played in the history of the lives of millions.

Communion and Witness

This is how you should pray:
    'Our Father, in heaven ...
    Your will be done ...' (Mt 6:9, 10)

FOR JESUS, THE WILL OF HIS HEAVENLY FATHER WAS HIS total focus. This will is spelled out for us in the wonderful lines: 'Lord Jesus, you were sent by the Father to gather together those who are scattered.'[57] This mission to gather the scattered was a matter of the heart for Jesus. When he looked on Jerusalem, a city at the centre of the life of his own people, he felt the full force of the mission he had been given by his heavenly father. Saint Matthew reports

---

56. Harris, *Lourdes: Body and Spirit in the Secular Age*, 2000, p. 366.

57. From the Prayer of the 50th International Eucharistic Congress, Dublin.

his stress: 'Jerusalem, Jerusalem, you that kill the prophets and stone those who are sent to you! How often have I longed to gather your children, as a hen gathers her chicks under her wings, and you refused!' (23:37). It is with that same longing that Jesus wants to gather his children in your parish and my parish and in every parish. It is in that context that we must read the daring words of Blessed John Paul to the whole Church at the beginning of this millennium: 'This is the other important area in which there has to be commitment and planning on the part of the universal Church and the particular Churches: the domain of communion (*koinonia*), which embodies and reveals the very essence of the mystery of the Church.'[58]

I discussed this concept of *koinonia* (or communion, or fellowship) earlier in the context of what God is offering us. With Blessed John Paul's insistence that here we are at what embodies and reveals the very essence of the Church, I want to focus on it again, this time in terms of what God is asking of us. Saint John exhorts us to: 'Think of the love that the Father has lavished on us, by letting us be called God's children and that is what we are. Because the world refused to acknowledge him, therefore it does not acknowledge us' (1 Jn 3:1). We are asked to allow ourselves be grasped by the familial love and identity into which we are plunged in baptism. Blessed John Paul was quite insistent as regards the fundamental nature of this challenge:

> To make the Church the home and school of communion: that is the great challenge facing us in

---

58. *Novo Millennio Ineunte*, 42.

the millennium which is now beginning, if we wish to be faithful to God's plan and respond to the world's deepest yearnings ...[59]

Blessed John Paul continues:

'By this love you have for one another, everyone will know that you are my disciples' (Jn 13:35). If we have truly contemplated the face of Christ, dear brothers and sisters, our pastoral planning will necessarily be inspired by the 'new commandment' which he gave us: 'love one another as I have loved you' (Jn 13:34).

So we need to do something new, to change from a certain kind of individual, maybe even a selfish ego-centred behaviour to a renewed life of belonging together. In this, Blessed John Paul warns that not only must we stir ourselves and do something, we must reflect prayerfully:

What does this mean in practice? Here too, our thoughts could run immediately to the action to be undertaken, but that would not be the right impulse to follow. Before making practical plans, we need to promote a spirituality of communion ... a spirituality of communion indicates above all the heart's contemplation of the Trinity dwelling in us ... A spirituality of communion also means an ability to think of our brothers and sisters in faith within the profound unity of the Mystical Body, and therefore as

---

59. Ibid., 43.

'those who are part of me'. A spirituality of communion 'makes us able to share their joys and sufferings, to sense their desires and attend to their needs, to offer them deep and genuine friendship.'[60]

We may ask what first steps we can take to 'make the Church the home and school of communion' or indeed what steps we can take to make our local Church the home and school of communion. I suggest that if you are a pilgrim you have already taken the first step. Your journey can be understood as an invitation to come and see what our Church is like when we prioritise our baptism into the Father, Son and Holy Spirit for even a few days and we see the light of the risen Christ in so many faces around us. I suggest a second step might be to share our faith in terms of discussing what we see and hear that encourages us. It is common for people to bring pious objects home from Lourdes for dear ones, in the hope that it will encourage their faith. A place like Lourdes can give us new interest in our faith and we want to share that. This is all well and good, but we must try and do a bit better. When it comes to faith we are not used to talking about the occasions when our hearts burn within us. We might frighten others and ourselves. Still, most of us who are baptised are also confirmed, and we are promised the help of the Holy Spirit in bearing witness to what we have seen and heard.

In 1961, Ireland celebrated a Patrician year to celebrate 1,500 years after the mission of St Patrick. A great crowd gathered at the Hill of Slane for a Mass to remember the lighting of the Easter fire for the first time among us. The young Fr Peter Connolly was the preacher. I think

60. Ibid.

his challenge still strikes a chord: 'Our special task is to overcome the old habit of silence or dumbness about our religion. We must, therefore, learn more and think more about our faith.'[61]

At the time of Bernadette, the parishioners of Lourdes were essentially forced to think and share their faith. They prayed, they shared, they acted, and with the Holy Spirit they helped to renew not only their own parish but far more than they could have imagined. Most parishes, even if they are already well-cultivated patches of ground, could produce bountiful fruit if the Word of God and the Holy Spirit were given more freedom to thrive. In a world scarred by loneliness, we need as many centres as possible where people can feel there is a place for them and their contribution.

A pilgrimage to Lourdes is an invitation to each person to 'come as you are', and bring all your needs and hopes, your hurts and pain. It is an invitation to recognise oneself as important in the eyes of God. It is an invitation to accept reconciliation and a new start, to recognise one's place in the family of God, in God's household. Hopefully your experience of the pilgrimage is also an experience of human companionship in a context of faith and prayer, an experience of living our baptismal identity together, living up to our identity as people clothed in Christ. At its best a pilgrimage helps us grasp, and be grasped by, a friendship with our Saviour Jesus Christ that we are invited to live with each other. This friendship that Our Saviour has lived with the Father and Holy Spirit for all

---

61. Tomás Ó Fiaich, eag., *Seanchas Ard Mhacha*: Journal of the Armagh Diocesan Historical Society, Documents of the Patrician Year, Armagh, 1962.

eternity and that he now shares with Mary and all the saints, is the same belonging and love into which we are all baptised, all plunged.

I once asked an elderly parishioner who was sad that her children and grandchildren were not Mass-goers: 'What happens when they do not go to Mass?' 'They forget,' she replied. I often think that what she said was very close to the mind of Christ at the Last Supper when he said: 'Do this in memory of me.' Gathering for Mass is the great gift Christ gave us to help us remember where we belong, to remind us of what he has said to us and receive the nourishment for the life that lasts. Of course, Mass is also the reminder that the return gift God asks of us is that we love one another and build up a body for him in our world today; a body that will be his love among the people of our time. Bernadette was given a task. She lived it as messenger to the priests – and to all – as witness to all of the recognition, respect, joy, beauty and friendship she experienced. Enough people in the parish of Lourdes were faithful witnesses to what they themselves had seen and heard. They bore witness in the face of ridicule and stiff opposition. They were part of enormous creativity.

Today we are asked to reflect on our experience of faith and generously share that experience with a grateful heart.

Baptism

THE ROSARY AND ITS MYSTERIES IS THE STORY THAT provides the context for the friendship of Bernadette and Mary. In a meditation on the rosary, Blessed John Paul reflected that when we contemplate the mysteries of the rosary we are attending a school where we can learn to contemplate the beauty of the face of Christ. He wrote that 'Each of the mysteries of light is a revelation of the Kingdom from now on present in the person of Jesus'.[62] The first Mystery of Light recalls the baptism of Jesus in the Jordan. We read in St Luke's gospel: 'When all the people had been baptised and while Jesus after his own baptism was at prayer, heaven opened and the Holy Spirit descended on him in bodily shape like a dove. And a voice came from heaven, "You are my Son, the Beloved; my favour rests on you"' (Lk 3:21, 22). Saint Luke presents this scene as the point where Jesus moves from his hidden life to his public life, a scene where Jesus receives in prayer and in the Holy Spirit the greatest celebration of who he is: the beloved Son, the one in whom the Father delights. Later on Jesus will say to his listeners: 'As the Father loves me so I have loved you', and 'Love one another as I have loved you'. It is the family love of the Father, Son and Holy Spirit that is the eternal wellspring of all that Jesus shares with us. Baptism is the act of being plunged into that river of love, into the life of the risen Christ.

Saint Paul tells us that in our baptism we put on Christ; we are clothed in Christ. In the early Church, the newly baptised were dressed in white, as a sign of this immersion in the life of the risen Christ, in the life of grace and family life of the Trinity. I think we need to renew our sense of the white coat of Christ as a sign of who we are as a people. Reflecting back on his experience of the great gathering in Croke Park for the final Eucharist of

---

62. *Rosarium Virginis Mariae*, 21.

the International Eucharistic Congress, a regular visitor to the same venue on sporting occasions said: 'It was my happiest day of all in Croke Park. We were all wearing the same jersey.' I could not help adding: 'We were all wearing one jersey, *cóta bán Chríost*.' So it is fitting that when we celebrate the friendship of St Bernadette and Mary, our Mother, that Mary appears as a lady dressed in white. She is dressed like all the baptised in the white coat of Christ. It is through the grace of Christ that Mary is full of grace. It was the deep conviction of Blessed John Paul that our prayer with Mary is a call to turn our attention to the person of Christ.

Bernadette's experience of recognition, respect, prayer and friendship opened up her own faith, hope and love in a whole new way. Bernadette was a sick young girl. Somehow her peace, joy and good heart were stronger than all her weakness. When we think of this and her ability to impact so positively on so many who probed every aspect of her mind, and indeed every aspect of her life, her community and her culture, we can ask: 'How could this be?' We can talk about many dimensions and provide various human stories. I think it is much more realistic to remember the answer Mary received at the first Joyful Mystery. The angel said to Mary: 'You are to conceive and bear a son, and you must name him Jesus. He will be great and be called Son of the Most High' (Lk 1:31-32). 'Mary said to the angel: "How can this come about, since I am a virgin?" "The Holy Spirit will come upon you," the angel answered' (Lk 1:34-35).

From the beginning of the story of Mary and Jesus, the power of the Holy Spirit is present. At the beginning of the story of the Church, the apostles 'joined in continuous prayer, together with several women, including Mary the mother of Jesus, and with his brothers', as they awaited the power of the Spirit to come at Pentecost. At the beginning of the story of the grotto of Lourdes, Bernadette heard the sound of the wind, and as she told her story to Fr Pomian, the chaplain in the hospice, two days later he immediately thought of the sound of the wind at Pentecost and the presence of the Holy Spirit. This might have been prompted by the fact that the bishop of the diocese, Mgr Laurence, had conferred Confirmation in the parish the previous week. These founding events of Lourdes were taking place among Christians, members of a Catholic parish and diocese. They lived their lives as members of the Church and of the People of God in that place at that time. They were heirs to a varied human heritage of languages and culture, including all the biblical heritage of the Old and New Testaments. As we try to renew our appreciation of the place of baptism in our lives as Christians, the words of Mary, 'Let what you have said be done to me' (Lk 1:38) ask us to pay attention to the prayer in the baptism ceremony that reads: 'The Lord Jesus made the deaf hear and the dumb speak. May he soon touch your ears to receive his word and your mouth to proclaim his faith, to the praise and glory of God the Father.'

When we pray these words we are surely taking on a responsibility to help this person hear the word of God. Mary says to us: 'Do whatever he tells you' (Jn 2:5). To be faithful to what we do at baptism and celebrate at Lourdes, we are asked to be people of the scriptures. The first Joyful Mystery, the Annunciation, celebrates Mary's welcome for the word of God and action of the Holy

Spirit. Baptism is our public acceptance of these sources of life.

A Spirituality of Truth and Solidarity

WHEN PREFECT MASSY WAS ON A VISIT TO LOURDES on 4 May, some weeks before the final apparition, he declared that anybody claiming to see a vision would be arrested. When Bernadette was told she might be put in prison, her response was simple: 'I do not fear anything because I have always told the truth.'[63] There is an amazing echo here of the trial of Jesus Christ before Pontius Pilate, when Jesus declared: 'Mine is not a kingdom of this world' (Jn 18:36). 'Yes, I am a King. I was born for this, I came into the world for this: to bear witness to the truth; and all who are on the side of truth listen to my voice' (Jn 18:37).

When we allow the Holy Spirit to touch our lives we must be prepared for new things. We can often be asked to let go of some ideas we took for granted. In the life of Bernadette, it was not just people in her parish and her diocese who had to make room in their heads for new ways of looking at their lives; new horizons had been opened up for a lot of people.

One thing that caused a lot of difficulties for Bernadette in her convent days was the fact that her superiors had some very definite ideas of what constituted 'holiness'. They wanted something much more conventional, something that lived up to their own expectations. It is easier for us now to recognise that in the life of

---

63. Laurentin, *Bernadette Vous Parle,* Tome X, 1972, p. 153.

Bernadette, the Holy Spirit and Bernadette were doing something new. Yes, Bernadette did not have any formal education. Her language was a minority language. We can list all the usual comments about why she is an 'enigma'. It might help if we take a broader view and remember what Jesus said to his friends: 'When they take you before synagogues, magistrates and authorities, do not worry about how to defend yourselves or what to say, because when the time comes, the Holy Spirit will teach you what to say' (Lk 12:11).

The examples of how her simple answers left critical questioners less sure of themselves go on and on. The day after her First Communion she was asked: 'What made you happier: your First Holy Communion or the apparitions?' Her simple reply was: 'They are two things that go together, but cannot be compared. I was happy both times.'[64] Then there is the story that shows Bernadette's clarity about her role as a Christian witness. A learned priest, who was later to become a bishop, told her he did not believe her story. She answered: 'I was not asked to make you believe. I was asked to tell you.'[65]

To say a wide variety of people to this day are fascinated by her composure and strong sense of self is to put it mildly. It gets more interesting when people express their amazement at her wisdom despite her lack of formal education or social status, in terms of her simplicity, of her age, even in terms of her lack of French. These remarks can contain all kinds of assumptions about formal education, social status, human simplicity and

---

64. Ravier, *Bernadette: The Saint of Poverty and of Light*, 1974, p. 25.

65. Chantal Touvet, *Tout Commença par un Souffle*, Nouan-Le-Fuzelier: Éditions des Béatitudes, 2008, p. 83.

even the need to speak good French! Patrick Kavanagh has an interesting comment here:

> No man need be a mediocrity if he accepts himself as God made him. God only makes geniuses. But many men do not like God's work. The poet teaches that every man has a purpose in life, if he would submit and serve it, that he can sit with his feet to the fire of an eternal passion, a valid moral entity.[66]

Kavanagh's sentiment is that the truth is what sets us free. Bernadette was learning that she had no need to become anything except herself as God was making her.

Reality and New Freedom
IN HIS POEM 'HAVING CONFESSED', PATRICK KAVANAGH says:

> God cannot catch us
> Unless we stay in the unconscious room
> Of our hearts. We must be nothing,
> Nothing that God may make us something.
> We must not touch the immortal material,
> We must not daydream tomorrow's judgement –
> God must be allowed to surprise us.[67]

I must admit I can struggle with sentiments that suggest we are nothing, but then I make peace with them when I see it in terms of giving up notions about our importance.

66. Patrick Kavanagh, *Collected Prose*, London: MacGibbon & Kee, 1967, p. 28.
67. Kavanagh, *Collected Poems*, 2004, p. 191.

Learning the truth about ourselves, accepting our real selves can involve humility, self-giving, suffering and a new freedom.

It gets very interesting when holiness, and wholeness, become a receiving of oneself from God in return for recognising his delight in us, recognising his self-giving love for us in that delight. Was not the self-assurance of Bernadette, her holiness, the wholeness of her humanity, nurtured by her friendship with the woman who sang: 'My soul proclaims the greatness of the Lord and my spirit exults in God my Saviour; because he has looked upon his lowly handmaid!' (Lk 1:46-48).

Saint Francis spoke of his experience that it is in giving that we receive. Then the words of Christ himself confirm this at its deepest: 'Anyone who finds his life will lose it; anyone who loses his life for my sake will find it' (Mt 10:39).

In her acceptance of herself as she is, and her abandonment to love, to friendship, in prayer and faith, Bernadette gives herself totally and she is receiving herself anew as a child of the Father and a sister to all Christ's sisters and brothers. With Mary she finds her place in the communion of saints. Her acceptance of her reliance on God allowed the Holy Spirit transform her into a person that puzzled the wise and the learned. She would have understood from experience the first words of Pope Benedict to young people in 2005:

If we let Christ into your lives, we lose nothing, nothing, absolutely of what makes life free, beautiful and great. No! Only in this friendship are the doors of life opened wide. Dear young people: do not be afraid of Christ! He takes nothing away and he gives you everything. When we give ourselves to him, we receive a hundredfold in return. Yes, open, open wide the doors to Christ – and you will find true life.[68]

At home, my father used to say to us with a big smile: 'Experience keeps a hard school, but fools will learn in no other.' He said it so gently that we never felt insulted. In fact, I tended to hear it as an echo of the psalm that says: 'Fools say in their hearts, "There is no God"' (53:1).

I have long been a student of Alexander Solzhenitsyn, feeling that any possible fruit that might have come from the terrible Soviet experiment, of which he was a victim, should not be wasted. One of the most extraordinary passages in all his writing is surely where he gives thanks to prison for all he has learned about life, humanity and divinity. Through all his suffering – his incarceration in a concentration camp, his bout of cancer – he saw himself moving into the light, from being a self-centred materialist to discovering a life-giving solidarity with the suffering and the rejected. Through accepting the loss of everything, being reconciled even to death, he came to a new understanding of himself.

Bernadette found a source of self, a source of wisdom, a source of human solidarity with the weakest that did not involve devotion to and worship of money. She was able to wonder at other things. Through her faith, her prayer, her daily life and her friendship, she and those who shared her journey increasingly became a cultivated ground where the fruits of the work of the Holy Spirit

---

68. Homily at the Mass for the Inauguration of the Pontificate, 2005.

nourished and continue to nourish the lives of millions. We can imagine the Lord saying to her what he said to his first disciples: 'I chose you; and I commissioned you to go out and to bear fruit, fruit that will last' (Jn 15:16). The risen Lord Jesus Christ, who was crucified, speaks these words to us too. He calls us to do more than 'add the halfpence to the pence/And prayer to shivering prayer'. The woman at the well is not the only one the Lord looks on with love and says: 'If you only knew what God is offering!' (Jn 4:10). The door into the 'more' that God is offering is the door of faith.

Faith

ONE STORY THAT TOUCHES MANY PEOPLE ON pilgrimage in Lourdes is about an Italian woman who lost her faith when her husband died tragically. One day she arrived in Lourdes as a tourist. She went to the grotto and surprised herself and everybody else by staying there for a long time. Soon she realised something had happened. She believed again. She was so filled with joy that the only image she could accept for what had happened to her was the story of Bartimaeus who was cured of his blindness by Jesus. She had a sculpture made with an inscription underneath reading: 'To recover faith is better than to recover sight.'[69]

Pope Benedict XVI insisted that faith is about a meeting with a person, a meeting with the Risen Christ who gives us a new perspective on life, a new way of seeing that transforms our consciousness. One paragraph in the

---

69. *The Wonders of Lourdes*, 2008, p. 255.

Pope's letter which launched the Year of Faith appeals to me as it refers to what makes our lives fruitful:

> Faith grows when it is lived as an experience of love received and when it is communicated as an experience of grace and joy. It makes us fruitful, because it expands our hearts in hope and enables us to bear life-giving witness: indeed, it opens the hearts and minds of those who listen to respond to the Lord's invitation to adhere to his word and become his disciples. Believers, so St Augustine tells us, 'strengthen themselves by believing'. The saintly Bishop of Hippo had good reason to express himself in this way. As we know, his life was a continual search for the beauty of the faith until such time as his heart would find rest in God.[70]

When we reflect on faith in our experience we are often drawn to the goodness we have known in the lives of people of faith. When we think about how people down through the years survived and lived with dignity and generosity through terrible times, we sense that their faith was a powerful resource. When we look at the 'enigma' of Bernadette we are drawn towards the faith she received in her home and in her parish. The Pope challenged us to learn more about the Christian faith: 'To rediscover the content of the faith that is professed, celebrated, lived and prayed, and to reflect on the act of faith, is a task that every believer must make his own ...'[71] He asks us not to separate love and faith, as they need each other:

---

70. *Porta Fidei*, 7.
71. Ibid., 9.

Faith without charity bears no fruit, while charity without faith would be a sentiment constantly at the mercy of doubt. Faith and charity each require the other, in such a way that each allows the other to set out along its respective path. Indeed, many Christians dedicate their lives with love to those who are lonely, marginalised or excluded, as to those who are the first with a claim on our attention and the most important for us to support, because it is in them that the reflection of Christ's own face is seen. Through faith, we can recognise the face of the risen Lord in those who ask for our love. 'In so far as you did this to one of the least of these brothers of mine, you did it to me.' These words are a warning that must not be forgotten and a perennial invitation to return the love by which he takes care of us.[72]

Lourdes has always been seen as a resource of faith and love. Because these two realities are so closely linked in the daily lives of pilgrims, they nourish each other. This link is lived out in a real companionship among those who might easily be labelled 'the sick and those caring for them'. That humble companionship is called to be a source of life, of love and faith for both, and a place where both grow in hope.

These realities of faith and a companioning love go right back to the very founding events of Lourdes. Another fundamental aspect of those founding events that I have emphasised is the way these people, most of whom had little formal education, talked to each other

---

72. Ibid., 14.

and to those who would listen. Despite their lack of formal education they were people of faith, and they spoke in a language of faith to each other. These days I think we are often faced with a great challenge in the area of language and faith.

As a help to meeting this challenge I suggest that the story of the two disciples on the road to Emmaus has a basic message to offer us (cf. Lk 24:13-35). On the first Easter Sunday, two of the disciples were leaving Jerusalem. They had no idea that the resurrection had taken place. They were full of disappointment at all the events of the previous week. On their journey, they were joined by a stranger who asked them what they were talking about. As they told him their story they used one phrase that always stands out for me: 'We had hoped ...' Then the stranger takes them on a journey through the scriptures to help them understand. At table that evening, 'at the breaking of bread', they recognised the stranger as their Risen Lord. As they hurried back to Jerusalem, they said to each other: 'Did not our hearts burn within us as he talked to us on the road, while he opened to us the Scriptures?'

As the Risen Christ was sending his disciples out to be his witnesses, he challenged them to read their own personal experiences in the light of the scriptures. The parishioners of Lourdes had to do a lot of reviewing of their experience in those first weeks, months and years. For many, including Bernadette, it was not at all clear what was being asked of them. They were like Mary, treasuring all these things, pondering them in their hearts. But through all that examination and reflection they gave so many a great message of hope, healing and new life. Through their conversations their faith and their experience met, and they found the words to give witness to so many. Now we are the Church, the Body of Christ, in this time and place. As children of the Church, as children of Mary, we too are asked to treasure the events that are our own personal experience as members of the family of Christ. We are all encouraged by the Risen Christ to re-read our lives in the light of the scriptures, like the disciples on the road to Emmaus. The parishioners of Lourdes and the faithful of the diocese of Tarbes have their call then and now. Through them, God is offering us the grace of a unique experience of the Church as the home and school of communion.

Lourdes, the Young, the Church

'MAKING NEW FRIENDS AND THINKING DIFFERENTLY' – this is what one young person took away from their pilgrimage to Lourdes. It is a voice of joy from the very heart of the story of Lourdes. There is something very liberating in the story of Bernadette for young people and their families who long to be recognised, even in their own eyes, as human beings with all the honour and respect that is due to any human being, even if they do not have wealth or health, social status or education. During a pilgrimage to Lourdes, young people feel a wonderful sense of liberation from all the pressures 'to be something that they are not'. We all want our young people to feel that we love them and want to cherish them as people in their own right. Adults and young people feel Lourdes helps us send the right messages to each other.

One of the particularly wonderful reports from the young at the end is how they talk about their involvement with the sick. So often they are nervous before meeting the sick and people in wheelchairs. But as they are with them on the way to and from the ceremonies, the baths, the Stations of the Cross, out in town shopping and at the singsongs, they find it all to be a great experience of faith and friendship.

At the end of five days they have an enormous sense of having made great discoveries in areas where they thought they knew all that was to be discovered. Their joy is often so great that they don't mind facing home with no explanation for their new attitudes to ordinary, everyday things. They just feel that if others really want to know, let them 'come and see', because 'you must experience it for yourself'. Every June, there are about one hundred young people on our diocesan pilgrimage. For them it is always an extraordinary experience of community, prayer and friendship, with a lot of fun mixed in. They lead a closing ceremony for the pilgrimage each year and our diocese rejoices in hope.

Some comments of the young people about the best part of the pilgrimage include:

'Getting to meet and make friends with so many people.'

'The procession and Mass at the grotto.'

'Meeting new people my age and interacting with the patients.'

'When I see the patients' faces light up when we talk to them and help. They really appreciate it. We only see this as something small but they really appreciate it.'

It is thought-provoking how much the young people find this experience of travelling together, in a faith atmosphere, such a wonderful opportunity for friendship. The fact that the whole experience is so intergenerational draws nothing but positive comments. The only problem in recruiting young people each year is that there are far more interested in coming than can be accommodated. Because young people want to experience what is on offer, we need to be able to say to them, and offer them opportunities to say to each other, 'come and see'.

Mary asked that people come in procession. The following testimony of one young Irish girl of her experience of the candlelight procession celebrates the response of millions over the years:

> Thousands of people from every nation across the world walk together, shoulder to shoulder; holding a candle and praying. By the time we reached the end the sun had just set and the candles are the only thing lighting. Then people raise their candles to the night sky in prayer, thanksgiving and honour to our Lord. It is magnificent and simply beautiful.[73]

At least two things are obvious: the faith of the Church and the Holy Spirit are definitely able to touch the lives of young people; and the lives of young people are open to the faith of the Church and the Holy Spirit.

The *National Directory for Catechesis in Ireland* speaking of young adults says: 'Opportunities must be provided to encourage them to celebrate and live their Christianity,

---

73. Aoife Daly 'Love Without Limit', Abbeyfeale Newsletter, Christmas 2012.

and come to know its fullest meaning in their lives and the significance of its contribution to the cultural world within which they live.'[74] The experience of young people in Lourdes is a sign of the possibilities that are open to us today. Places like Lourdes and Taizé stand alongside the World Youth Days as glimpses of the positivity of young people and faith.

Already But Not Yet ...

AT THE THIRD APPARITION BERNADETTE WAS TOLD by her new friend: 'I do not promise to make you happy in this world but in the other.'[75] Still, even if Bernadette did not know the fullness of happiness in this world, things had changed. The experience of the apparitions and the new awareness of her faith and its personal nature gave her a whole new grasp on life. She knew that she was not just a 'sick ignorant girl'. She knew she could trust her new friend to make her happy after all the suffering. For her, grace had already given her a new life but it was not yet the fullness of joy.

This is the reality for every Christian. In baptism we are plunged into a new life of the faith of the Christian community. This faith tells us that through baptism, in some mysterious way, we enter into the death of Christ and his risen life enters into us so that we become children of God, like Jesus. It can be hard to get our heads around this. Saint John in his first letter offers us a focus:

---

74. Irish Episcopal Conference, *Share the Good News: National Directory for Catechesis in Ireland*, Dublin: Veritas, 2011, p. 111.

75. Laurentin, *Bernadette Vous Parle*, Tome X, 1972, p. 49.

You must see what great love the Father has lavished on us by letting us be called God's children – which is what we are! The reason why the world does not acknowledge us is that it did not acknowledge him. My dear friends, we are already God's children, but what we shall be in the future has not yet been revealed. We are well aware that when he appears we shall be like him, because we shall see him as he really is. (1 Jn 3:1-2)

In the life of every baptised Christian there is an 'already but not yet'. In our celebration of the Easter mysteries and at every Mass as we celebrate the memorial of the death and resurrection of Jesus Christ, we celebrate the hope that in a real way we are already members of the Risen Christ as well as praying to be faithful until he comes again. This is usually described as the tension of the inbetween time, the 'already but not yet' of salvation. At every Mass we recall that we are blessed to be invited to the Supper of the Lamb, the great banquet of heaven. Pope Benedict presented the real life-giving power of Christian hope in his encyclical letter on that topic:

'SPE SALVI facti sumus' – in hope we were saved, says Saint Paul to the Romans, and likewise to us (Rm 8:24). According to the Christian faith, 'redemption' – salvation – is not simply a given. Redemption is offered to us in the sense that we have been given hope, trustworthy hope, by virtue of which we can face our present: the present, even if it is arduous, can be lived and accepted if it leads towards a goal, if we can be sure of this goal ...[76]

Here too we see as a distinguishing mark of Christians the fact that they have a future: it is not that they know the details of what awaits them, but they know in general terms that their life will not end in emptiness. Only when the future is certain as a positive reality does it become possible to live the present as well. So now we can say: Christianity was not only 'good news' – the communication of a hitherto unknown content. In our language we would say: the Christian message was not only 'informative' but 'performative'. That means: the Gospel is not merely a communication of things that can be known – it is one that makes things happen and is life-changing. The dark door of time, of the future, has been thrown open. The one who has hope lives differently; the one who hopes has been granted the gift of a new life.[77]

We might say that Bernadette was given a special grace to strengthen her hope in her sufferings. Yes, but we are asked to follow her confidence through the love lavished on us.

The French poet Charles Péguy presented the dynamic role of hope in the life of God's people who are animated by the great virtues of faith, hope and charity:

What really surprises me, says God, is hope.
This little girl who has the air of being nothing at all.

---

76. *Spe Salvi*, 1.

77. Ibid., 2.

She steps out, between her two big sisters,
And no one notices her at all.
One big sister is the faithful wife,
The other is the mother,
And my Christian people have a regard only for the
grown ups
And they hardly notice at all the little one in the
middle,
The one still going to school,
And who gets caught in the skirts of the older ones
When she walks with them.
And they believe that it is the two big ones who are
carrying the
Young one along by the hand,
In the middle,
Between them
To help her along the rough road of salvation.
The blind, they do not see that
It is the little one in the middle who is carrying her
two big sisters along.
And that without her they would be nothing,
But two women of a certain age,
Crushed by life.
It is herself, the little one, who carries everyone along.[78]

So many who come to Lourdes receive fresh heart. They
make so many references to heaven that while they know
they are not yet there, they do have a sense that heaven
has already come near. It was so from the very beginning.
Recently I was making a monthly communion call to a

---

78. Charles Péguy, *Le Porche du Mystère de la deuxième vertu*, Paris:
Librairie Hachette, 1952, p. 29. M. Liston trans.

parishioner when I asked her carer about Lourdes. She told me how: 'A few of us went down very early in the morning, about 5.30 a.m., to the grotto. We were able to get up near Our Lady, leave our petitions and an offering. We sat down and said some prayers. It was beautiful, so peaceful. The sun was beginning to shine. I couldn't explain it. It was like heaven.' As a comment on the grotto, she spoke for millions.

My Kingdom is Not of this World

AT THE TRIAL OF CHRIST, THE ROMAN PREFECT Pontius Pilate represented the powers of this world. Our Lord acknowledged that he was a king but that his kingdom was not of this world (cf. Jn 18:36). If his kingdom were of this world his men would have fought to save him. Bernadette also accepted that the happiness she was promised was not to be found in this world. However, the goodness and the joy she found here strengthened her for the struggles of the journey of salvation. Through Mary she was led to a deeper companionship with the Risen Christ into the fullness of life.

On his visit to Lourdes in September 2008, Pope Benedict in his talk with the sick said:

Today Mary dwells in the joy and the glory of the Resurrection. The tears shed at the foot of the cross have been transformed into a smile which nothing can wipe away, even as her maternal compassion towards us remains unchanged ... To seek Mary's smile is not an act of devotional or outmoded sentimentality, but rather the proper expression of the living and profoundly human relationship which binds us to her whom Christ gave us as our Mother.[79]

Even in the joy of the Annunciation the hope of salvation was alive. At the birth of the Lord, the angels spoke of good news, joy for all the people. The Second Vatican Council tells us that the inner nature of the Church is now made known to us through various images.[80] One of these images is that 'the Church is a tract of land to be cultivated, the field of God (1 Cor: 3-9)'.[81] I started this story of Lourdes by describing what happened when new potential in one under cultivated field was recognised and people responded. Lourdes in 1858 was already producing fruit. Still, in the light of what happened since, we see that in 1858 it was under-cultivated. Each one of us, and every community, parish and diocese that we belong to, has potential, is an under-cultivated field. May the example of Mary and Bernadette encourage us to recognise and respond to what the Spirit is saying to us now, in our place.

---

79. Benedict XVI, *Lourdes: Love is the True Cure*, London: Catholic Truth Society, 2009, p. 35.

80. Cf. *Lumen Gentium*, 6.

81. *The Documents of Vatican II*, London/Dublin: Geoffrey Chapman/ Veritas, 1966.

Possible Questions to Support a Review of Life

When we are taking a faith look at the events in our lives, we are invited to go beyond the usual questions asked at the end of a pilgrimage: 'Did you like it?' and 'Would you go again?' It is important to look deeper at what we actually experienced rather than just judging it in terms of whether it was a 'nice part of the holiday' or not. Painful experiences, even if we are not anxious to relive them, can be rich sources of learning.

This review is an invitation to look at our lives together and see where the Lord is calling us. Its basic elements are:

› A sharing of actual lived experiences, of personal hopes, fears, disappointments and joys – the reality of the actual lives of particular people

› A care for each other in friendship

› An atmosphere of faith that recognises that this is a looking with love at the action of God in our lives, with the help of the scriptures

› A call to conversion, to what is best in us, to commit ourselves anew to taking part in God's plan of love for people, to issue a response to Mary's call for penance, and to change our hearts.

What practical steps can we take at the end of our pilgrimage – or any time we share something that touches us deeply – to 'treasure all these things and ponder them in our hearts' as sincere friends of Mary? How can we walk together, talking about these recent events in our lives, sharing how words of faith were stirred in our hearts and minds?

We could help people revisit their experience, as the Risen Christ did with his disciples on the road to Emmaus, by inviting them to see what God is doing in their lives:

› How did you come to be involved on this pilgrimage to Lourdes?
› What difference has it made to you or to others?
› When do you do as Mary did, and ponder on these things that you have experienced here?
› Where does God speak to your faith?
› Was there any event or word in these days that was a grace for you?

Bernadette and her fellow parishioners were witnesses to what they saw and heard.

› When we go home, can we be witnesses to what we have experienced? Can we do things a bit differently when we get home?
› Is the Spirit of Jesus asking us to do something so that others will know God's love in a new way?

SOURCES AND BIBLIOGRAPHY

Actes du Colloque de 'l'Année Bernadette', Bruyères-le-Châtel: Nouvelle Citè, 2009

Béguin, Albert, *Bernanos par lui-même*, Paris: Éditions du Seuil, 1958

Benedict XVI, *Spe Salvi*, Encyclical Letter, 30 November 2007

——, *Lourdes: Love is the True Cure*, London: Catholic Truth Society, 2009

——, *Porta Fidei*, Apostolic Letter, 11 October 2011

Billet, Bernard and René Laurentin, *Lourdes: Documents Authentique* (seven vols, 1956–66), Paris: Lethielleux, 1956–66

Catechism of the Catholic Church, London/Dublin: Geoffrey Chapman/ Veritas, 1994

Chivot, Dominique, *Et Lourdes Pour Vous?*, Paris: Lethielleux, 2007

Conneely, Daniel, *The Letters of St Patrick*, An Daingean: An Sagart, 1993

Daly, Aoife, 'Without Limit', Abbeyfeale Newsletter, Christmas 2012

Espace Bernadette Soubirous Nevers, *Some of Bernadette's Sayings*, Nevers: Saint-Gildard's Convent, 1978

Harris, Ruth, *Lourdes: Body and Spirit in the Secular Age*, London: Penguin, 2000

John Paul II, *Redemptor Hominis*, Encyclical Letter, 4 March 1979

——, *Novo Millennio Ineunte*, Apostolic Letter, 6 January 2001

——, *Rosarium Virginis Mariae*, Apostolic Letter, 16 October 2002

Kavanagh, Patrick, *Collected Poems*, Antoinette Quinn, ed., London: Allen Lane, 2004

——, *Collected Prose*, London: MacGibbon & Kee, 1967

Korson, Gerald, ed., *The Wonders of Lourdes: 150 Miraculous Stories of the Power of Prayer to Celebrate the 150th Anniversary of Our Lady's Apparition*, New York: Magnificat, 2008

Laurentin, René, *Bernadette of Lourdes*, London: Darton, Longman & Todd, 1979

——, *Lourdes: Histoire Authentique des Apparitions*, Paris: Lethielleux, 1961

——, *Bernadette Vous Parle*, Lourdes: Oeuvre de la Grotte, 1972

Lefebvre-Filleau, Jean-Paul, *L'Affaire Bernadette Soubirous*, Paris: Cerf, 1997

Lourdes magazine@lourdes.org

Ó Floinn, Críostóir, *Three French Saints: Bernadette Soubirous*, Dublin: Columba Press, 2009

Ó Ríordáin, Seán, *Na Dánta*, Gaillimh: Cló Iar-Chonnacht, 2012

Paul VI, *Gaudium et Spes*, Pastoral Constitution on the Church in the Modern World, 7 December 1965

Péguy, Charles, *Le Porche du Mystère de la deuxième vertu*, Paris: Gallimard, 1952

Perrier, Jacques, *Bernadette, pourquoi je l'aime*, Lourdes: NDL Editions, 2009

——, ed., *Bernadette, de Lourdes à Nevers: actes du Colloque de 'L'Année Bernadette' (Lourdes, 8-10 Décembre 2008)*, Bruyères-le-Châtel: Nouvelle Cité, 2009

Point, René, *Servir les Malades à Lourdes 1885–1985, 100 ans d'Hospitalité*, Lourdes: NDL Éditions, 2009

Ravier, André, *Bernadette: The Saint of Poverty and of Light*, Paris: Nouvelle Librairie de France, 1974

——, *Bernadette d'après ses lettres*, Paris: Lethielleux, 1979

Seanchas Ard Mhacha: Journal of the Armagh Diocesan Historical Society, Documents of the Patrician Year, Tómás Ó Fiaich, eag., Armagh, 1962

The Fraternity of Little Sisters of Jesus, *Following Brother Charles of Jesus, 'The Universal Little Brother'*, Rome, 1975

Touvet, Chantal, *Tout Commença par un Souffle*, Nouan-Le-Fuzelier: Éditions des Béatitudes, 2008